OPEN SEASON

Writer: Daniel Way

Penciler: Bart Sears

Inker: Mark Pennington
Colorist: Mike Atiyeh
Letterers: Virtual Calligraphy's Cory Petit
& Chris Eliopoulos
Cover Artist: Paolo Rivera
Editor: Warren Simons
Executive Editor: Axel Alonso

Collections Editor: Jeff Youngquist
Assistant Editor: Jennifer Grünwald
Book Designer: Jeof Vita
Creative Director: Tom Marvelli

Editor in Chief: Joe Quesada
Publisher: Dan Buckley

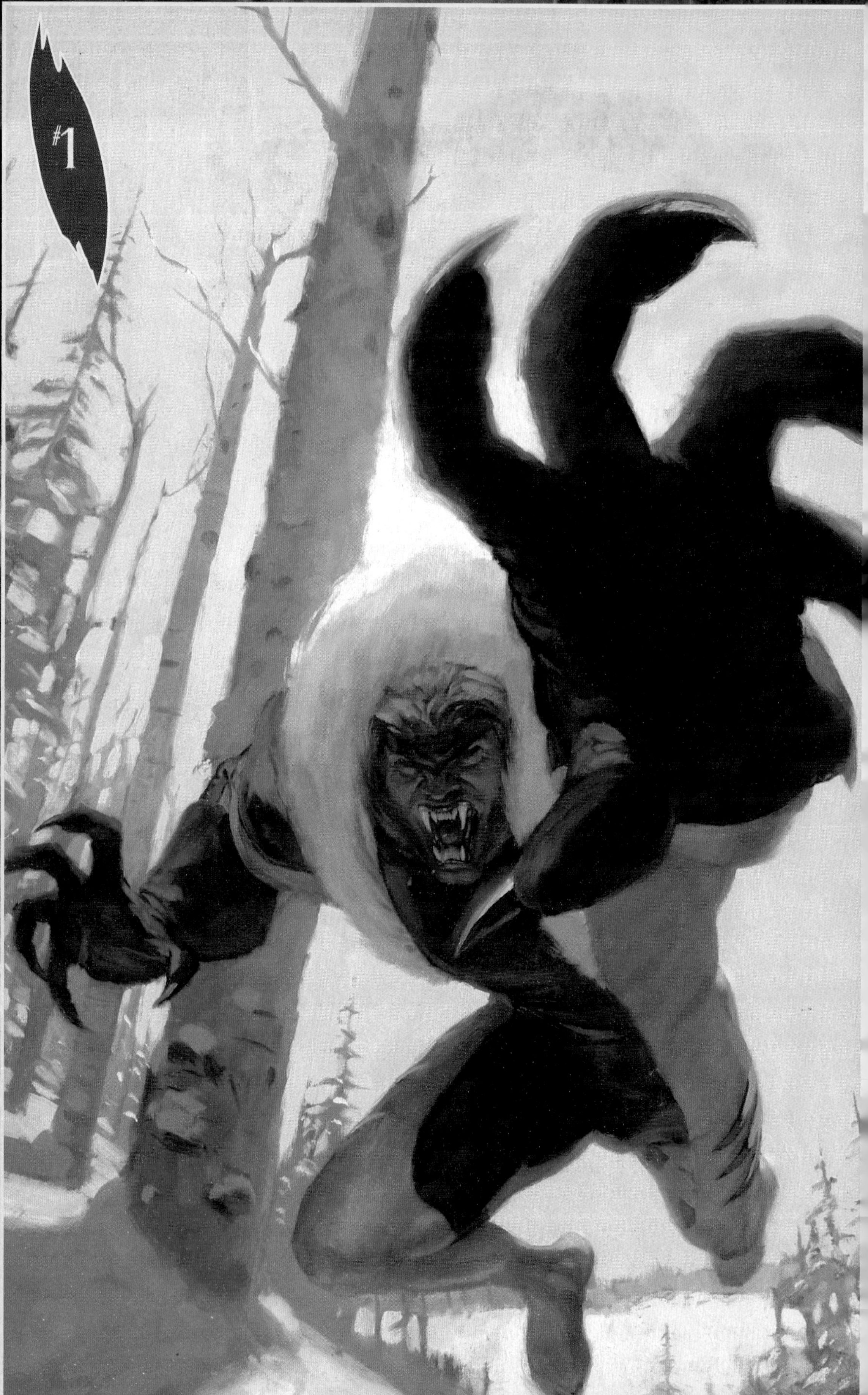
#1

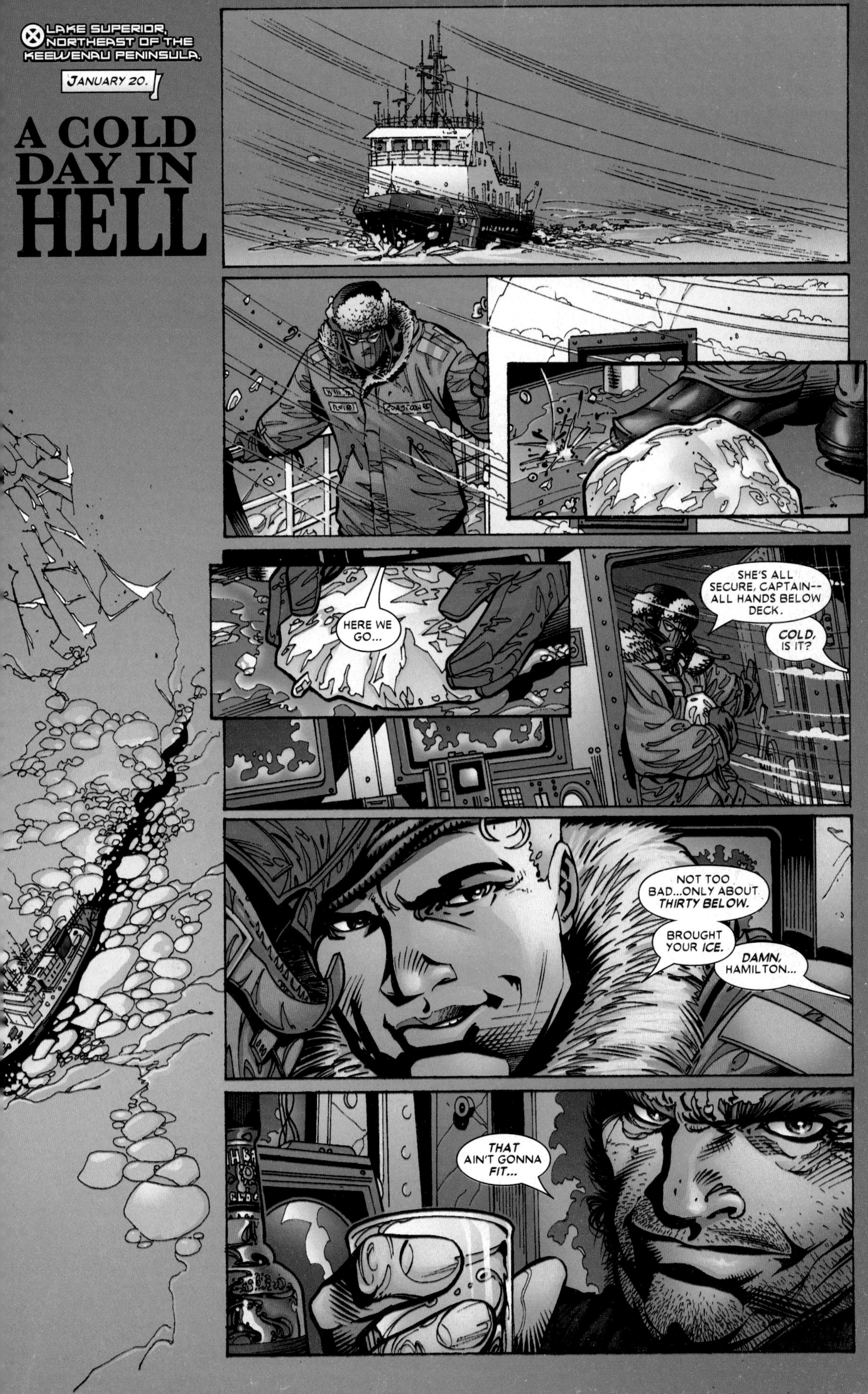
LAKE SUPERIOR, NORTHEAST OF THE KEEWENAU PENINSULA.
JANUARY 20.
A COLD DAY IN HELL
HERE WE GO...
SHE'S ALL SECURE, CAPTAIN--ALL HANDS BELOW DECK.
COLD, IS IT?
NOT TOO BAD...ONLY ABOUT THIRTY BELOW.
BROUGHT YOUR ICE.
DAMN, HAMILTON...
THAT AIN'T GONNA FIT...

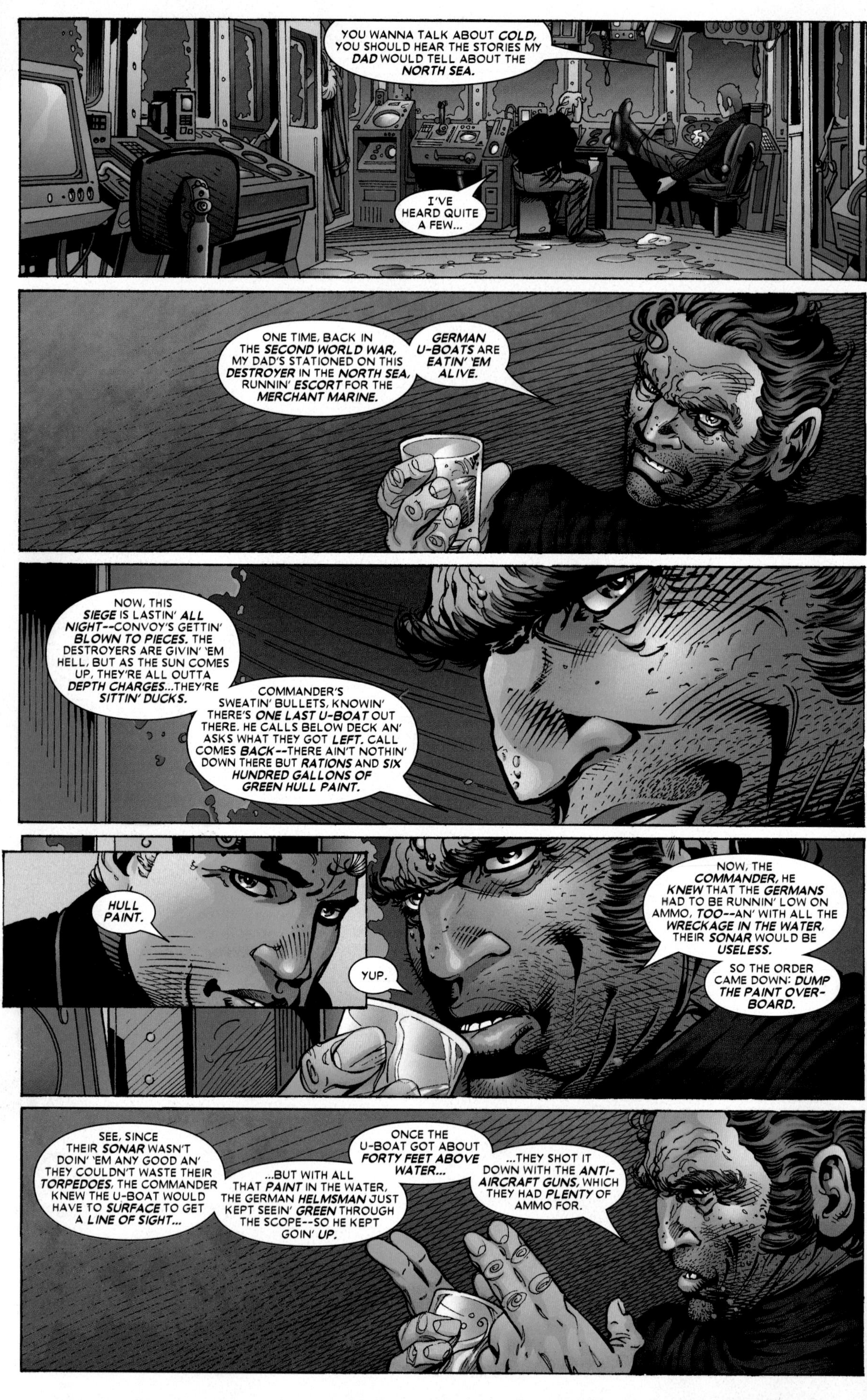

YOU WANNA TALK ABOUT COLD, YOU SHOULD HEAR THE STORIES MY DAD WOULD TELL ABOUT THE NORTH SEA.
I'VE HEARD QUITE A FEW...
ONE TIME, BACK IN THE SECOND WORLD WAR, MY DAD'S STATIONED ON THIS DESTROYER IN THE NORTH SEA, RUNNIN' ESCORT FOR THE MERCHANT MARINE.
GERMAN U-BOATS ARE EATIN' 'EM ALIVE.
NOW, THIS SIEGE IS LASTIN' ALL NIGHT--CONVOY'S GETTIN' BLOWN TO PIECES. THE DESTROYERS ARE GIVIN' 'EM HELL, BUT AS THE SUN COMES UP, THEY'RE ALL OUTTA DEPTH CHARGES...THEY'RE SITTIN' DUCKS.
COMMANDER'S SWEATIN' BULLETS, KNOWIN' THERE'S ONE LAST U-BOAT OUT THERE. HE CALLS BELOW DECK AN' ASKS WHAT THEY GOT LEFT. CALL COMES BACK--THERE AIN'T NOTHIN' DOWN THERE BUT RATIONS AND SIX HUNDRED GALLONS OF GREEN HULL PAINT.
HULL PAINT.
YUP.
NOW, THE COMMANDER, HE KNEW THAT THE GERMANS HAD TO BE RUNNIN' LOW ON AMMO, TOO--AN' WITH ALL THE WRECKAGE IN THE WATER, THEIR SONAR WOULD BE USELESS.
SO THE ORDER CAME DOWN: DUMP THE PAINT OVER-BOARD.
SEE, SINCE THEIR SONAR WASN'T DOIN' 'EM ANY GOOD AN' THEY COULDN'T WASTE THEIR TORPEDOES, THE COMMANDER KNEW THE U-BOAT WOULD HAVE TO SURFACE TO GET A LINE OF SIGHT...
...BUT WITH ALL THAT PAINT IN THE WATER, THE GERMAN HELMSMAN JUST KEPT SEEIN' GREEN THROUGH THE SCOPE--SO HE KEPT GOIN' UP.
ONCE THE U-BOAT GOT ABOUT FORTY FEET ABOVE WATER...
...THEY SHOT IT DOWN WITH THE ANTI-AIRCRAFT GUNS, WHICH THEY HAD PLENTY OF AMMO FOR.

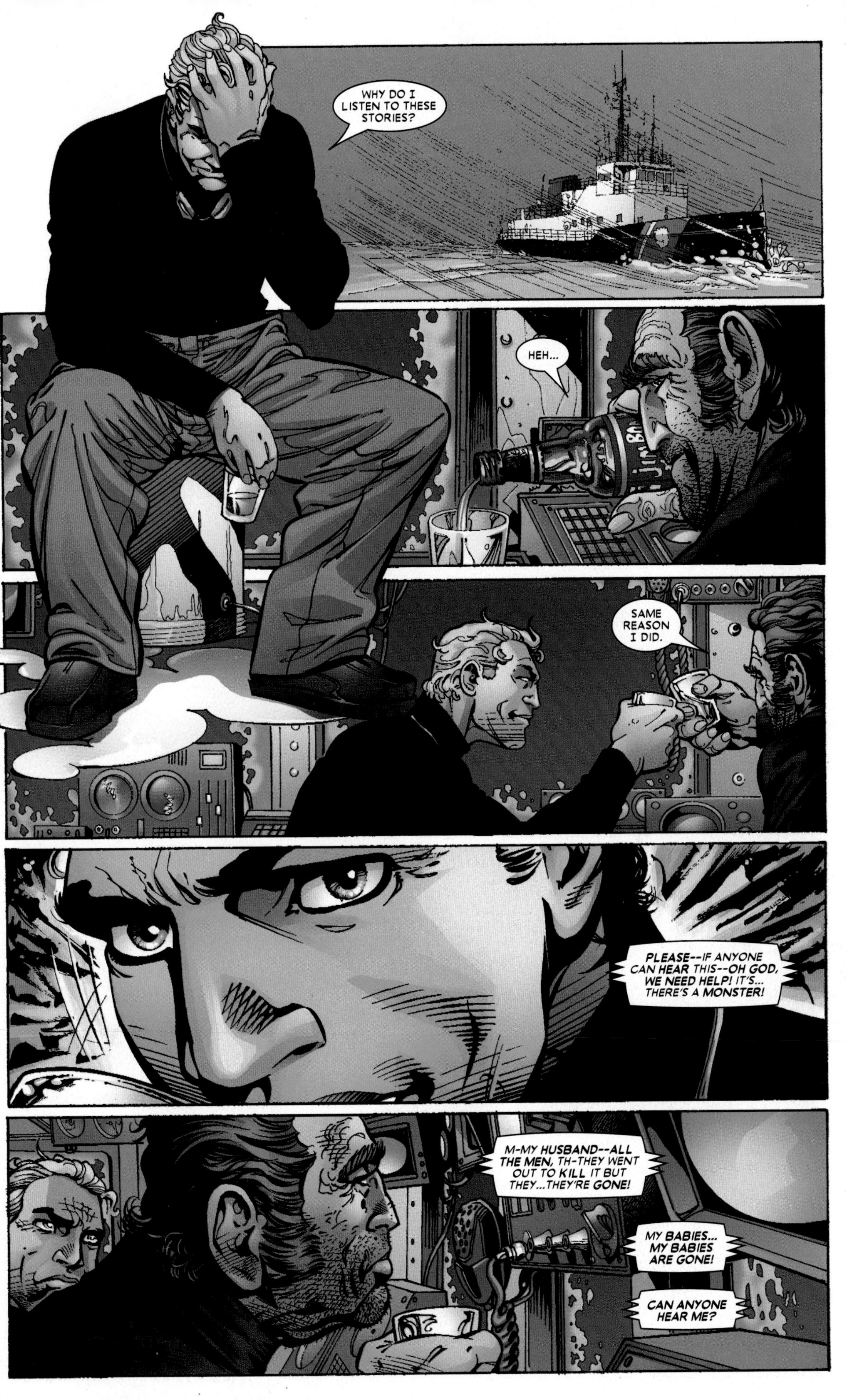
WHY DO I LISTEN TO THESE STORIES?
HEH...
SAME REASON I DID.
PLEASE--IF ANYONE CAN HEAR THIS--OH GOD, WE NEED HELP! IT'S... THERE'S A MONSTER!
M-MY HUSBAND--ALL THE MEN, TH-THEY WENT OUT TO KILL IT BUT THEY...THEY'RE GONE!
MY BABIES... MY BABIES ARE GONE!
CAN ANYONE HEAR ME?

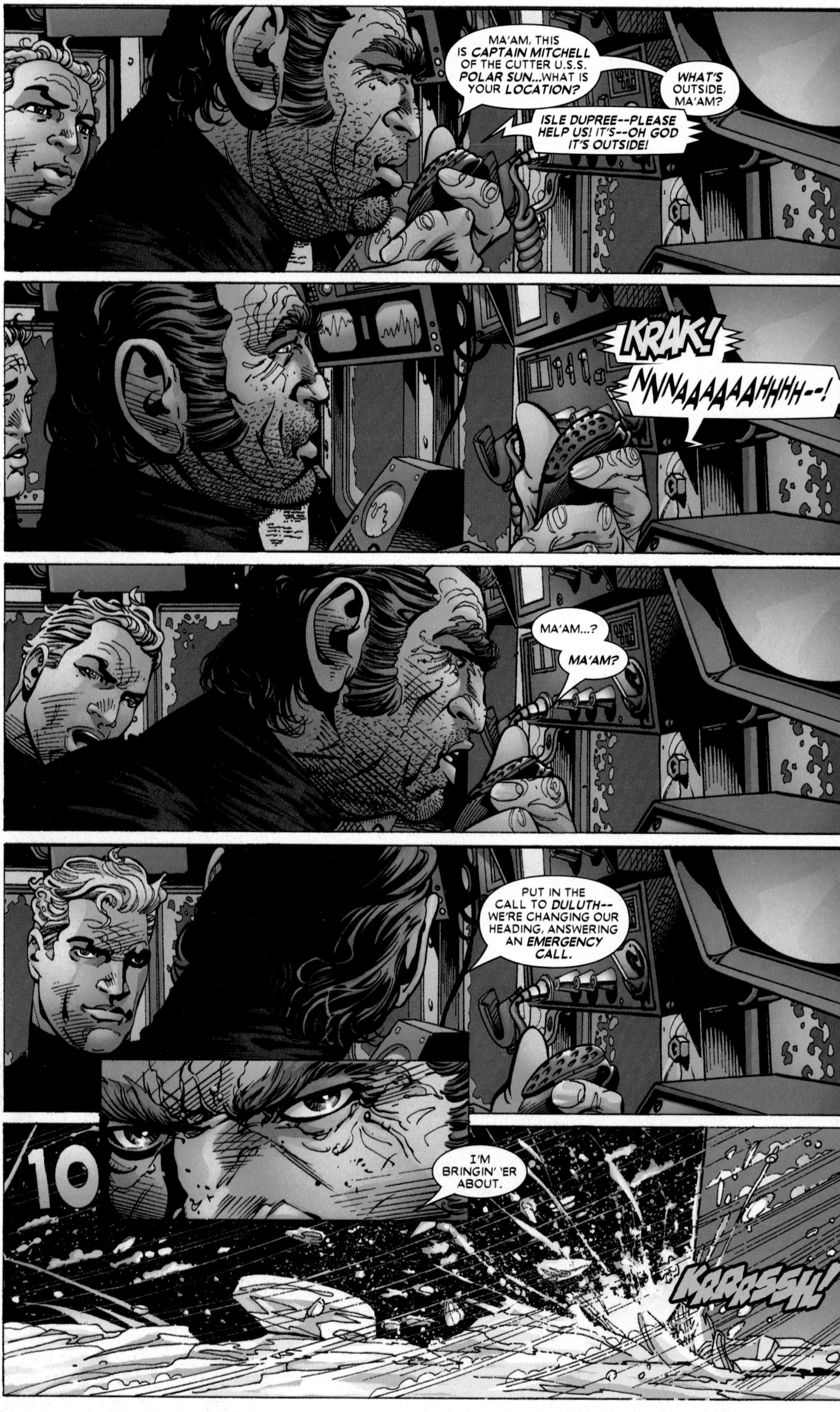
MA'AM, THIS IS CAPTAIN MITCHELL OF THE CUTTER U.S.S. POLAR SUN...WHAT IS YOUR LOCATION?
WHAT'S OUTSIDE, MA'AM?
ISLE DUPREE--PLEASE HELP US! IT'S--OH GOD IT'S OUTSIDE!
KRAK!
NNNAAAAAAHHHH--!
MA'AM...?
MA'AM?
PUT IN THE CALL TO DULUTH--WE'RE CHANGING OUR HEADING, ANSWERING AN EMERGENCY CALL.
10
I'M BRINGIN' 'ER ABOUT.
KRRRSSH!

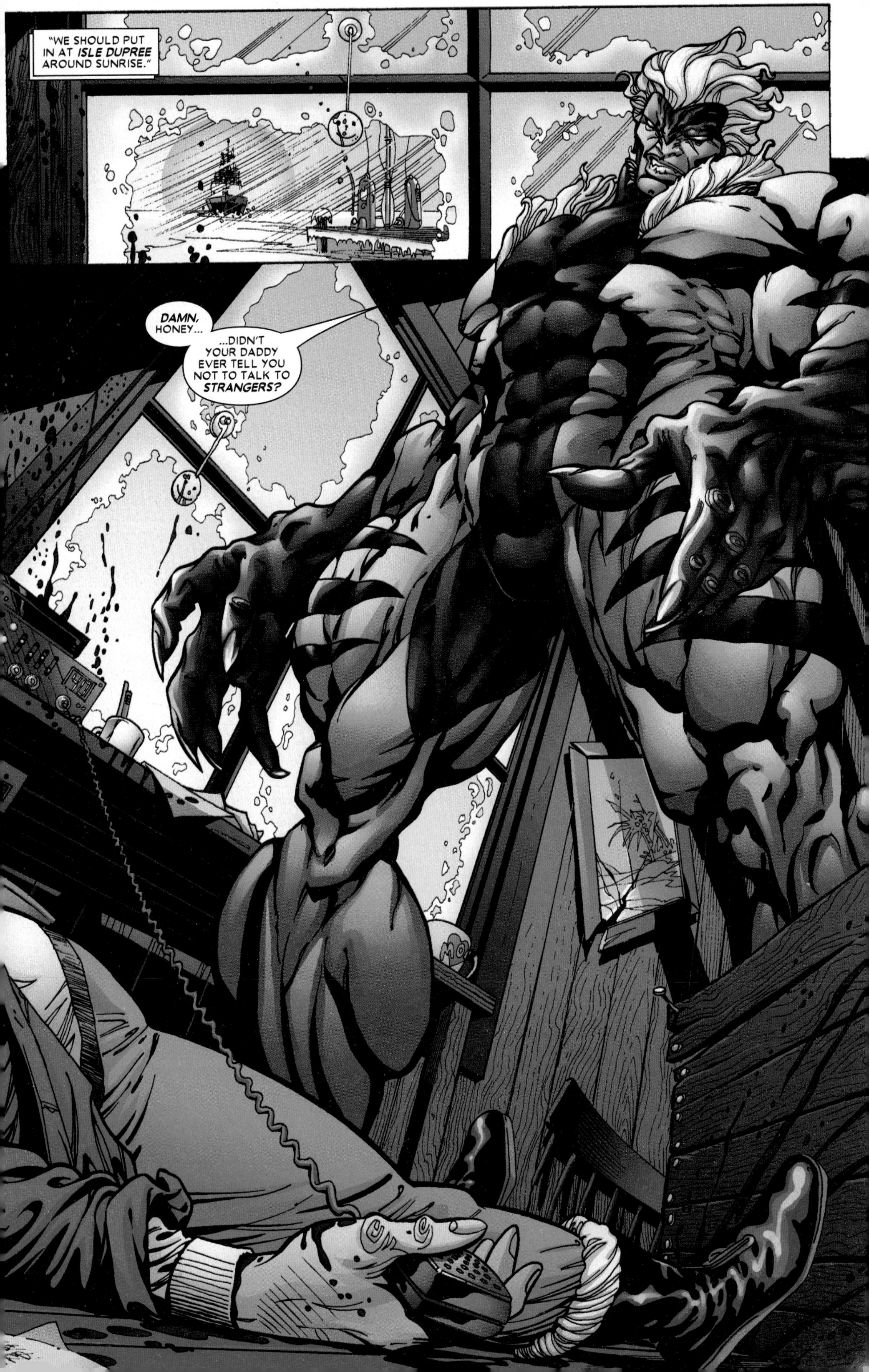
"WE SHOULD PUT IN AT ISLE DUPREE AROUND SUNRISE."
DAMN, HONEY...
...DIDN'T YOUR DADDY EVER TELL YOU NOT TO TALK TO STRANGERS?

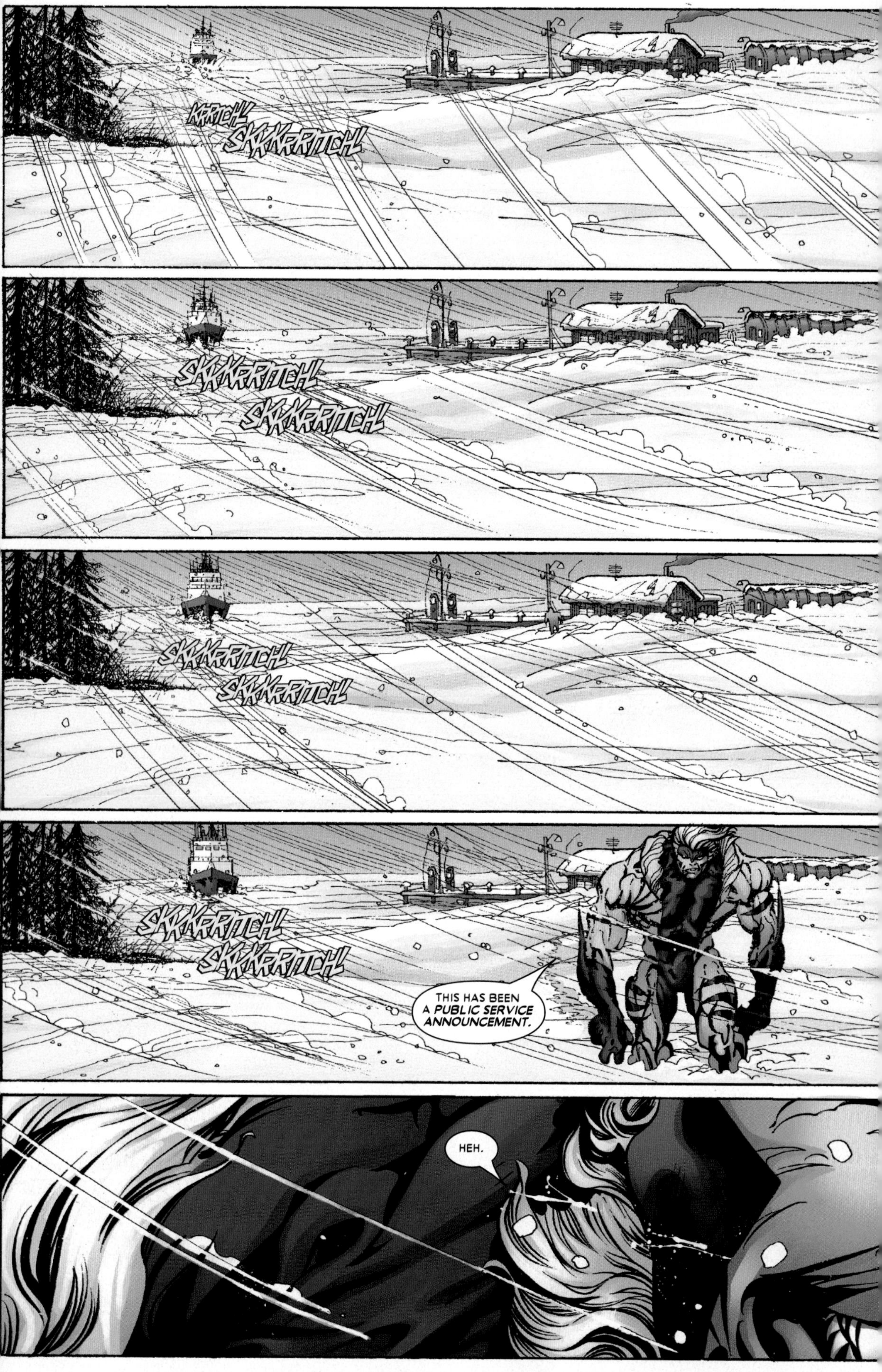
KRRTCH!
SKKKRRITCH!
SKKKRRITCH!
SKKKRRITCH!
SKKKRRITCH!
SKKKRRITCH!
SKKKRRITCH!
SKKKRRITCH!
THIS HAS BEEN A PUBLIC SERVICE ANNOUNCEMENT.
HEH.

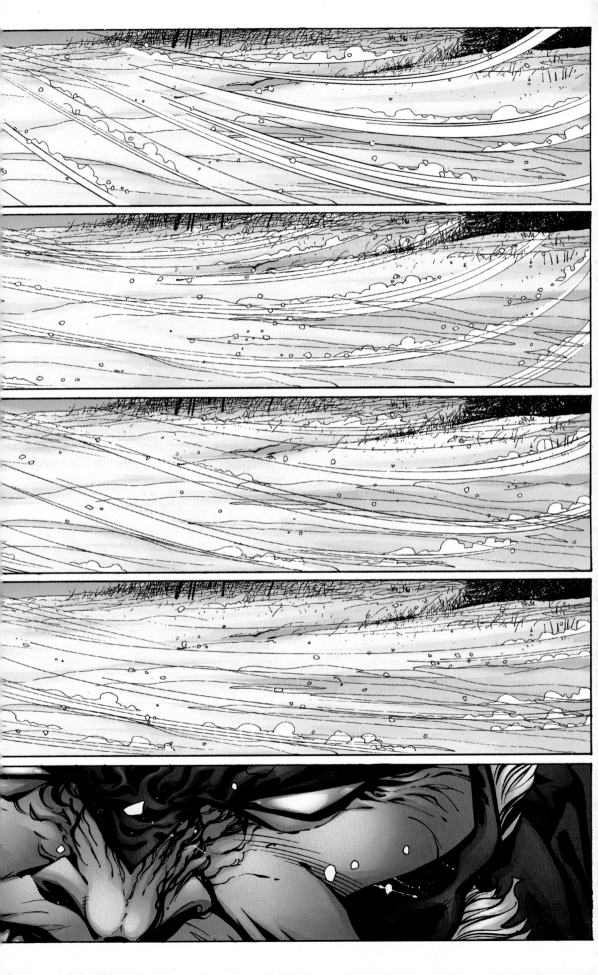

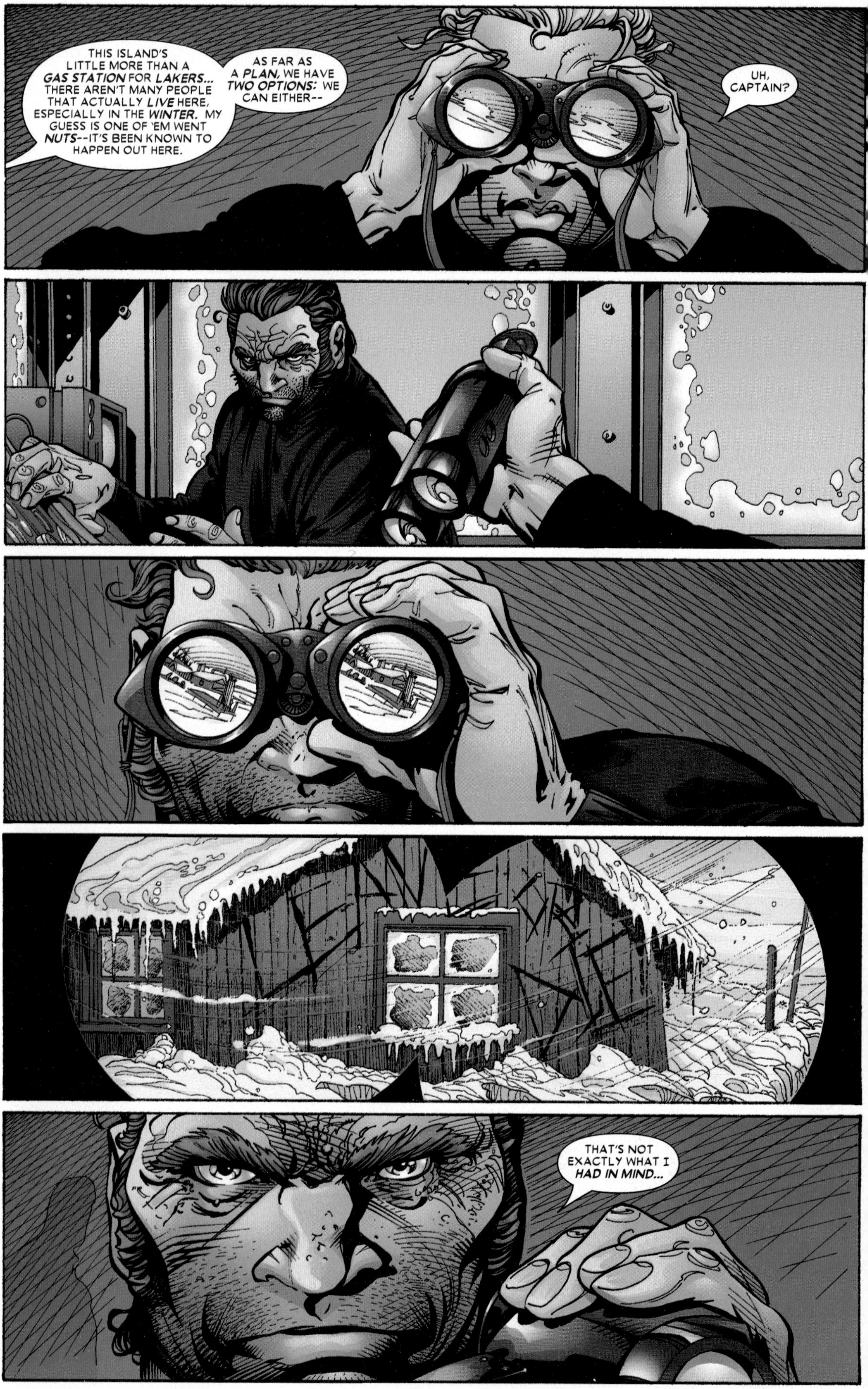
THIS ISLAND'S LITTLE MORE THAN A GAS STATION FOR LAKERS... THERE AREN'T MANY PEOPLE THAT ACTUALLY LIVE HERE, ESPECIALLY IN THE WINTER. MY GUESS IS ONE OF 'EM WENT NUTS--IT'S BEEN KNOWN TO HAPPEN OUT HERE.
AS FAR AS A PLAN, WE HAVE TWO OPTIONS: WE CAN EITHER--
UH, CAPTAIN?
THAT'S NOT EXACTLY WHAT I HAD IN MIND...

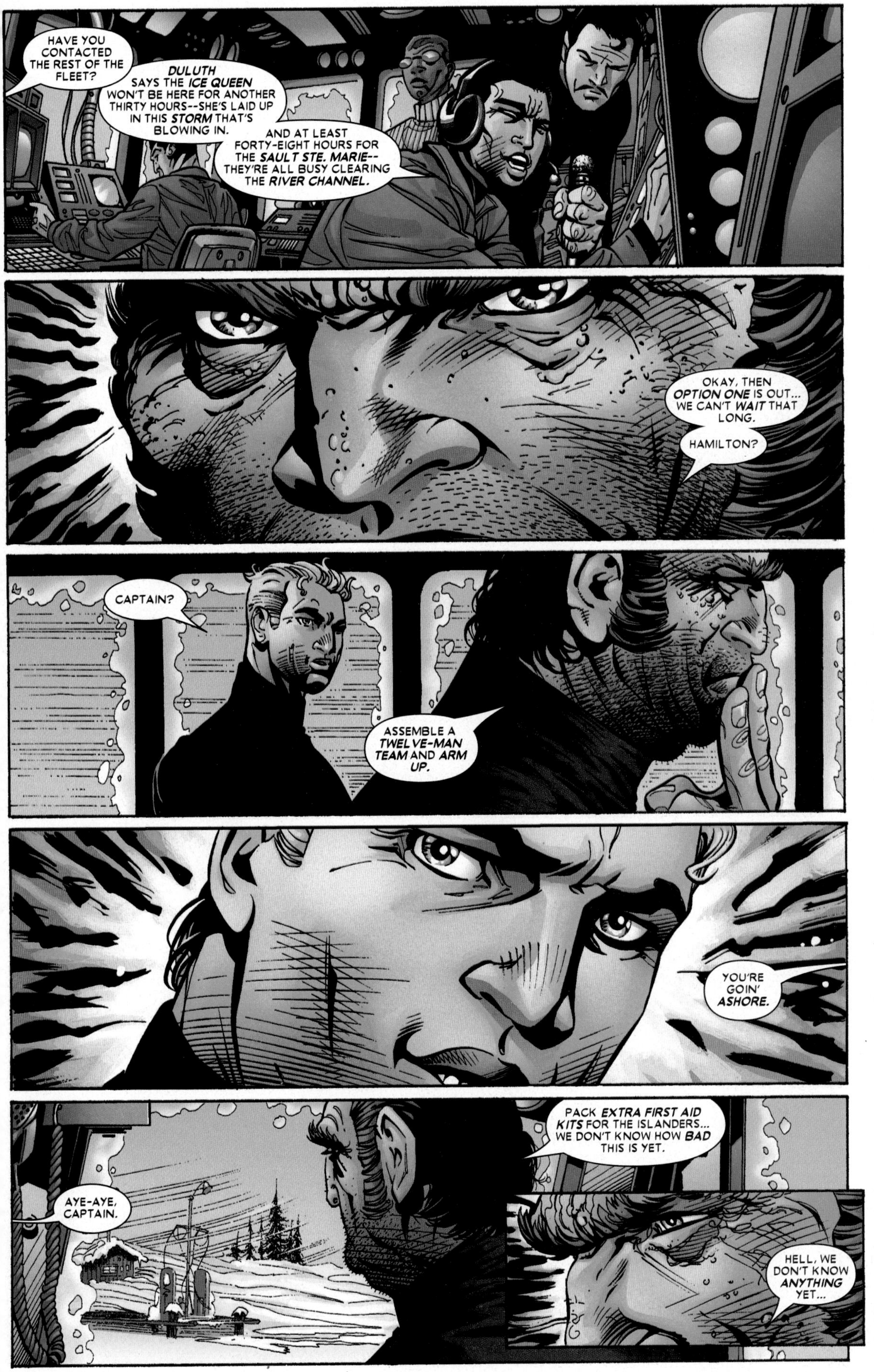
HAVE YOU CONTACTED THE REST OF THE FLEET?
DULUTH SAYS THE ICE QUEEN WON'T BE HERE FOR ANOTHER THIRTY HOURS--SHE'S LAID UP IN THIS STORM THAT'S BLOWING IN.
AND AT LEAST FORTY-EIGHT HOURS FOR THE SAULT STE. MARIE-- THEY'RE ALL BUSY CLEARING THE RIVER CHANNEL.
OKAY, THEN OPTION ONE IS OUT... WE CAN'T WAIT THAT LONG.
HAMILTON?
CAPTAIN?
ASSEMBLE A TWELVE-MAN TEAM AND ARM UP.
YOU'RE GOIN' ASHORE.
PACK EXTRA FIRST AID KITS FOR THE ISLANDERS... WE DON'T KNOW HOW BAD THIS IS YET.
AYE-AYE, CAPTAIN.
HELL, WE DON'T KNOW ANYTHING YET...

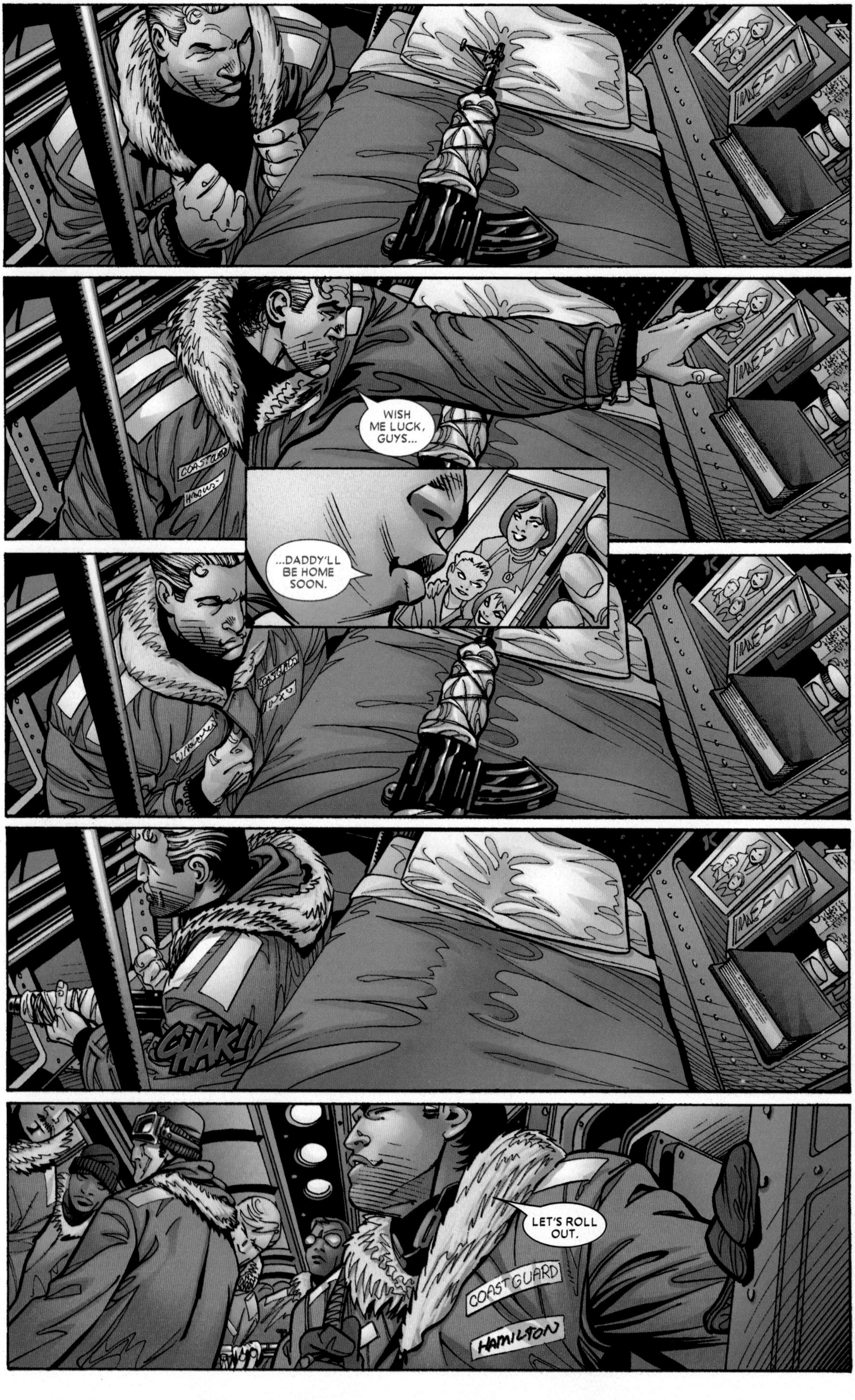
WISH ME LUCK, GUYS...
...DADDY'LL BE HOME SOON.
CHAK!
LET'S ROLL OUT.
COAST GUARD
HAMILTON

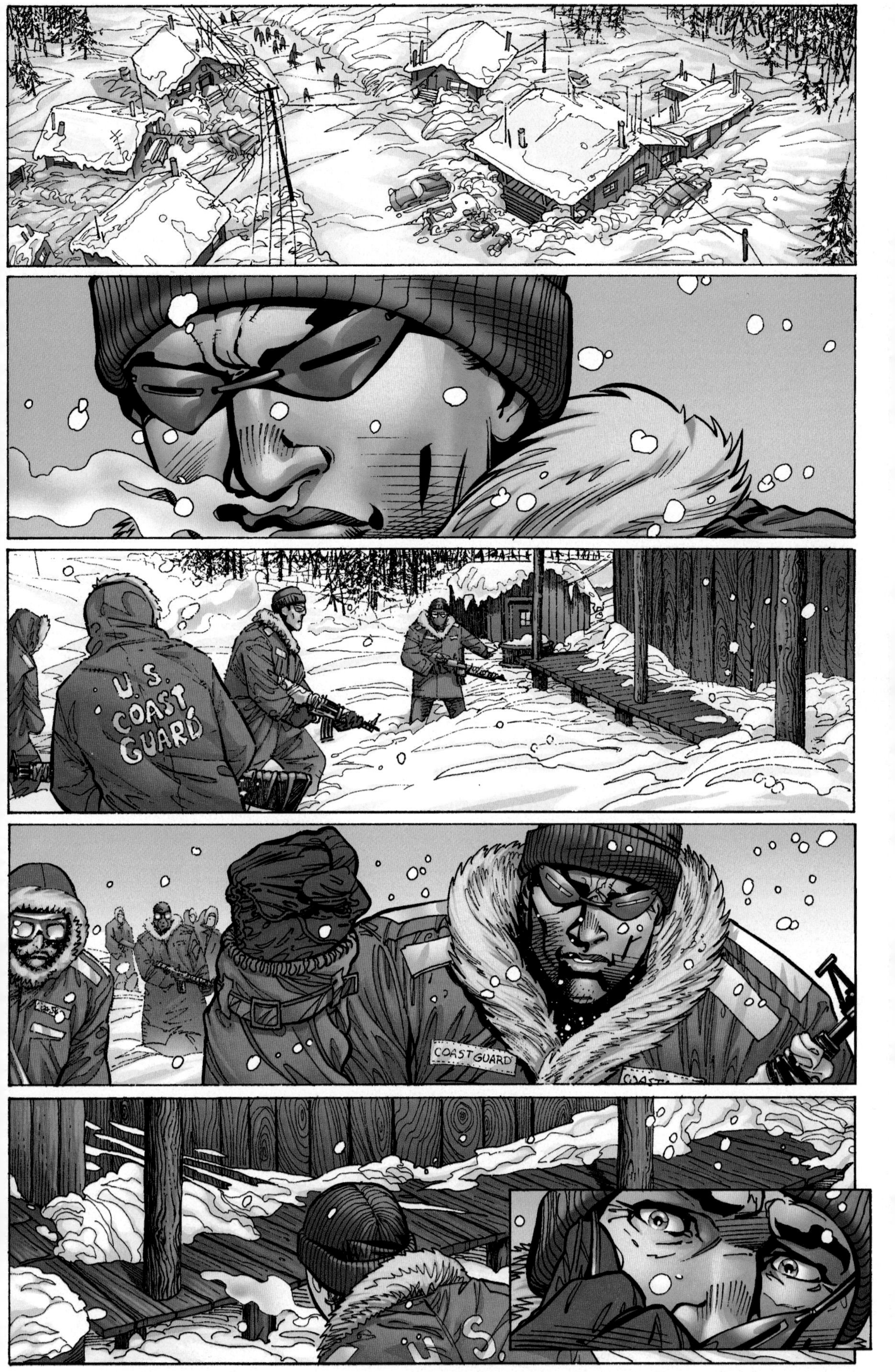
U.S.
COAST
GUARD
COASTGUARD

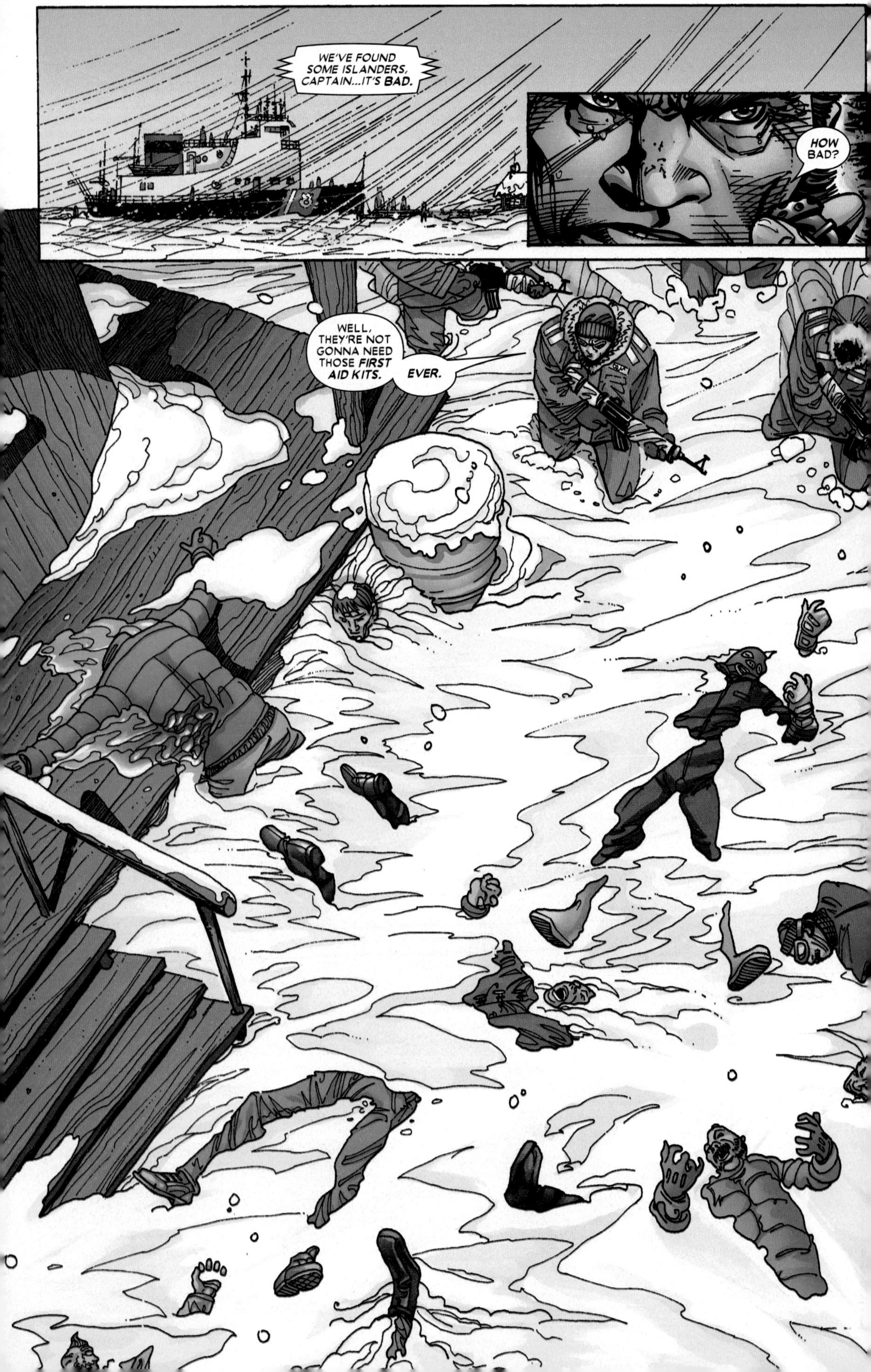
WE'VE FOUND SOME ISLANDERS, CAPTAIN...IT'S BAD.
HOW BAD?
WELL, THEY'RE NOT GONNA NEED THOSE FIRST AID KITS.
EVER.

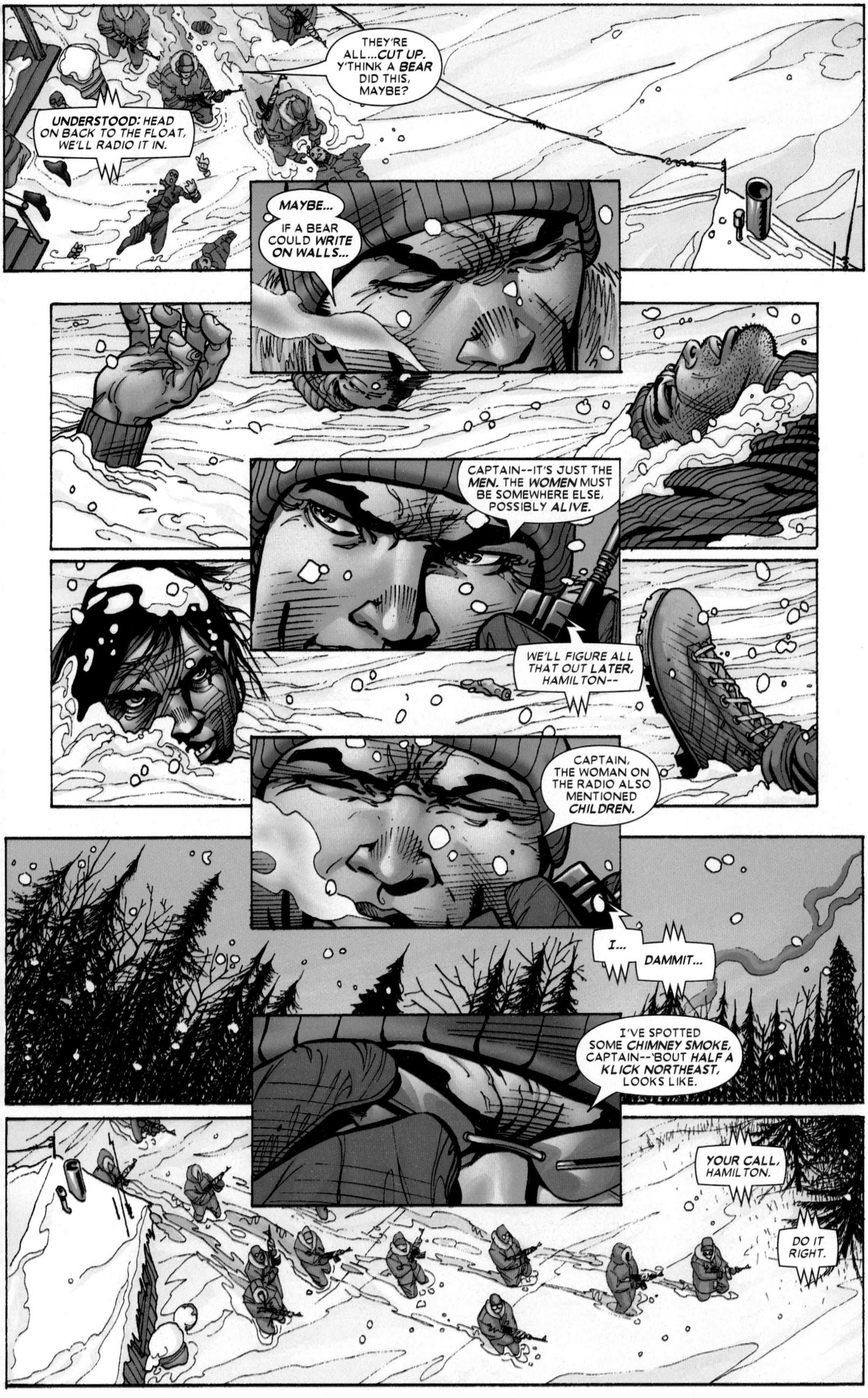
THEY'RE ALL...CUT UP. Y'THINK A BEAR DID THIS, MAYBE?
UNDERSTOOD: HEAD ON BACK TO THE FLOAT, WE'LL RADIO IT IN.
MAYBE...
IF A BEAR COULD WRITE ON WALLS...
CAPTAIN--IT'S JUST THE MEN. THE WOMEN MUST BE SOMEWHERE ELSE, POSSIBLY ALIVE.
WE'LL FIGURE ALL THAT OUT LATER, HAMILTON--
CAPTAIN, THE WOMAN ON THE RADIO ALSO MENTIONED CHILDREN.
I...
DAMMIT...
I'VE SPOTTED SOME CHIMNEY SMOKE, CAPTAIN--'BOUT HALF A KLICK NORTHEAST, LOOKS LIKE.
YOUR CALL, HAMILTON.
DO IT RIGHT.

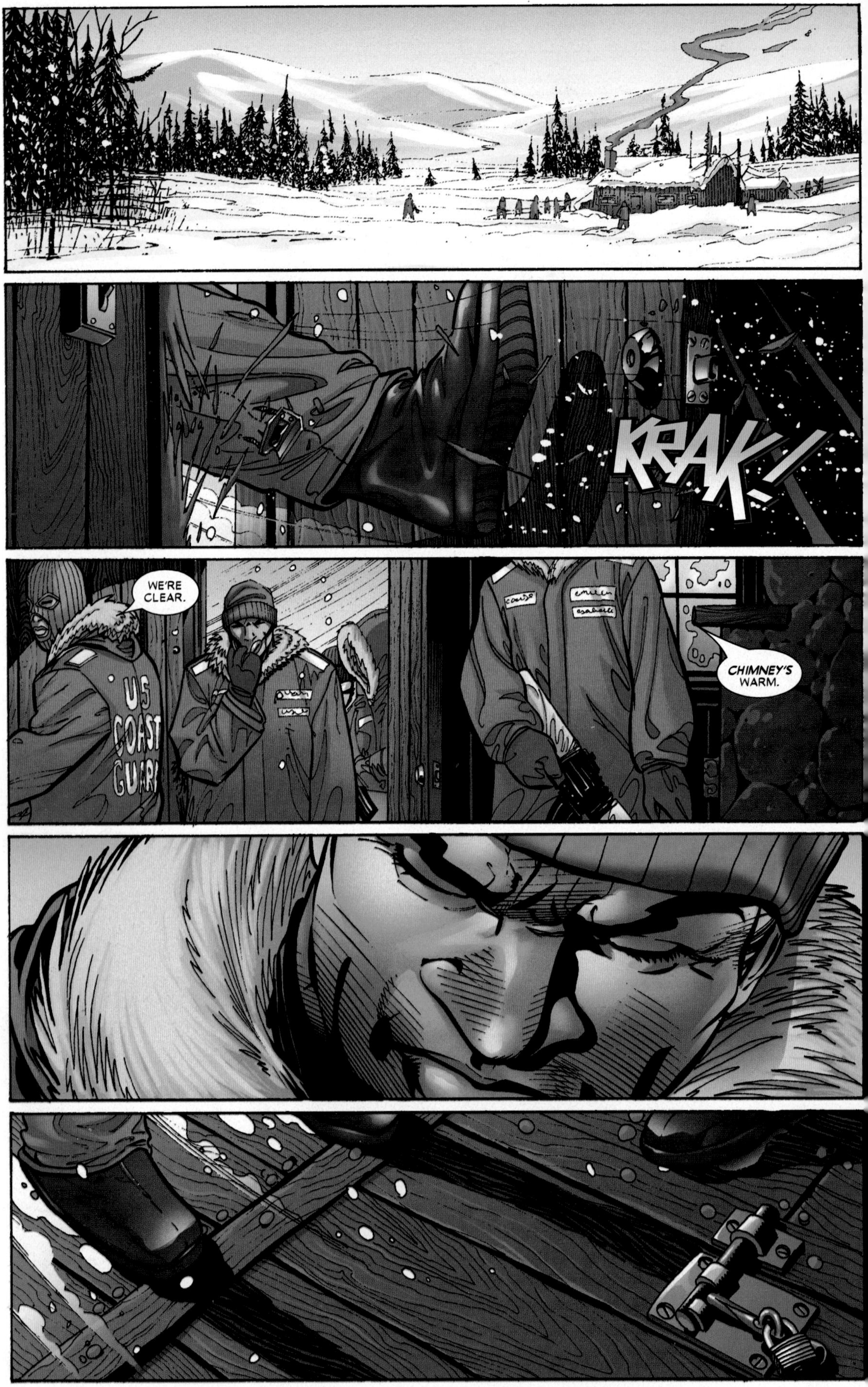
KRAK!
WE'RE CLEAR.
US COAST GUARD
CHIMNEY'S WARM.

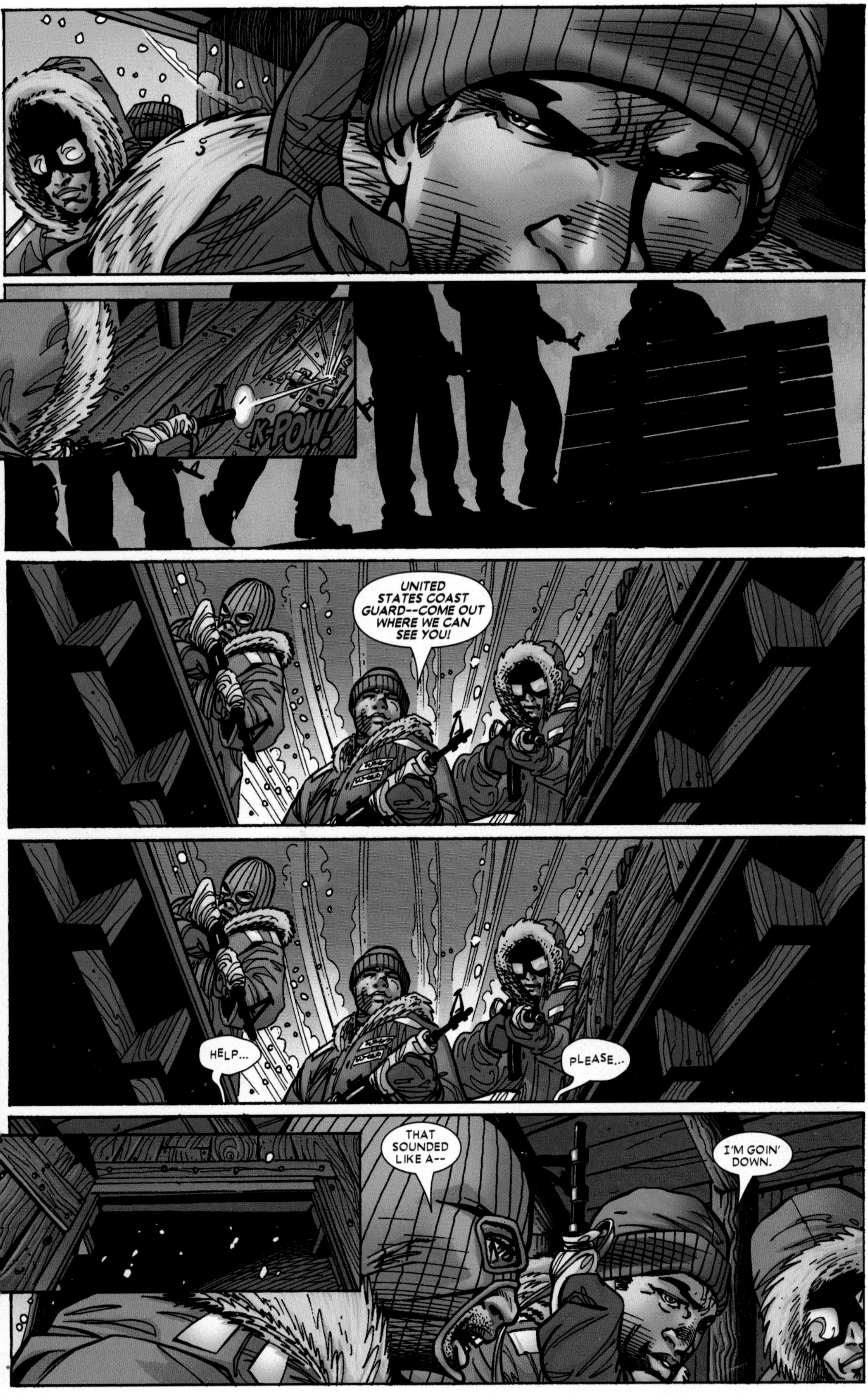
K-POW!
UNITED STATES COAST GUARD--COME OUT WHERE WE CAN SEE YOU!
HELP...
PLEASE...
THAT SOUNDED LIKE A--
I'M GOIN' DOWN.

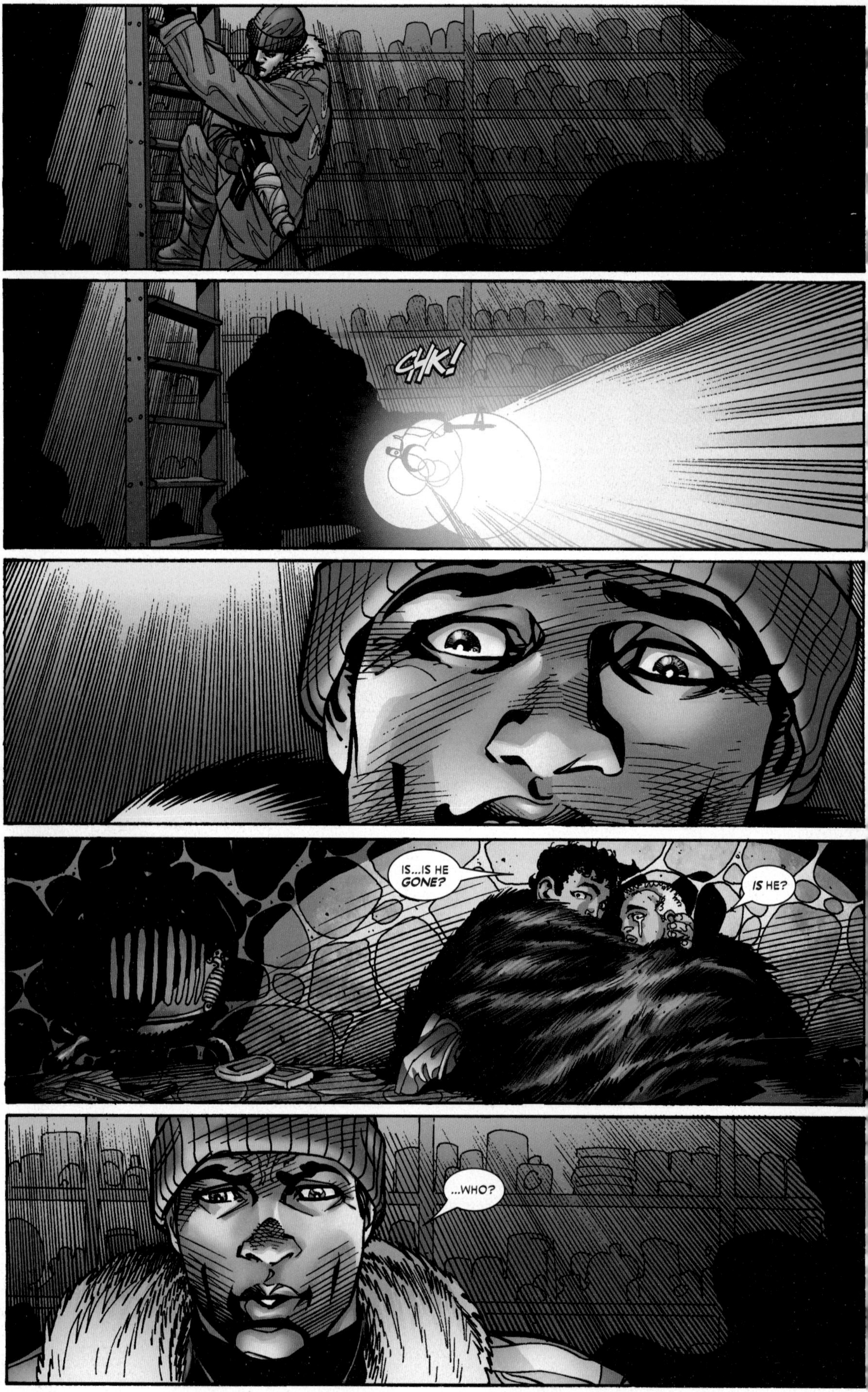
CHK!
IS...IS HE GONE?
IS HE?
...WHO?

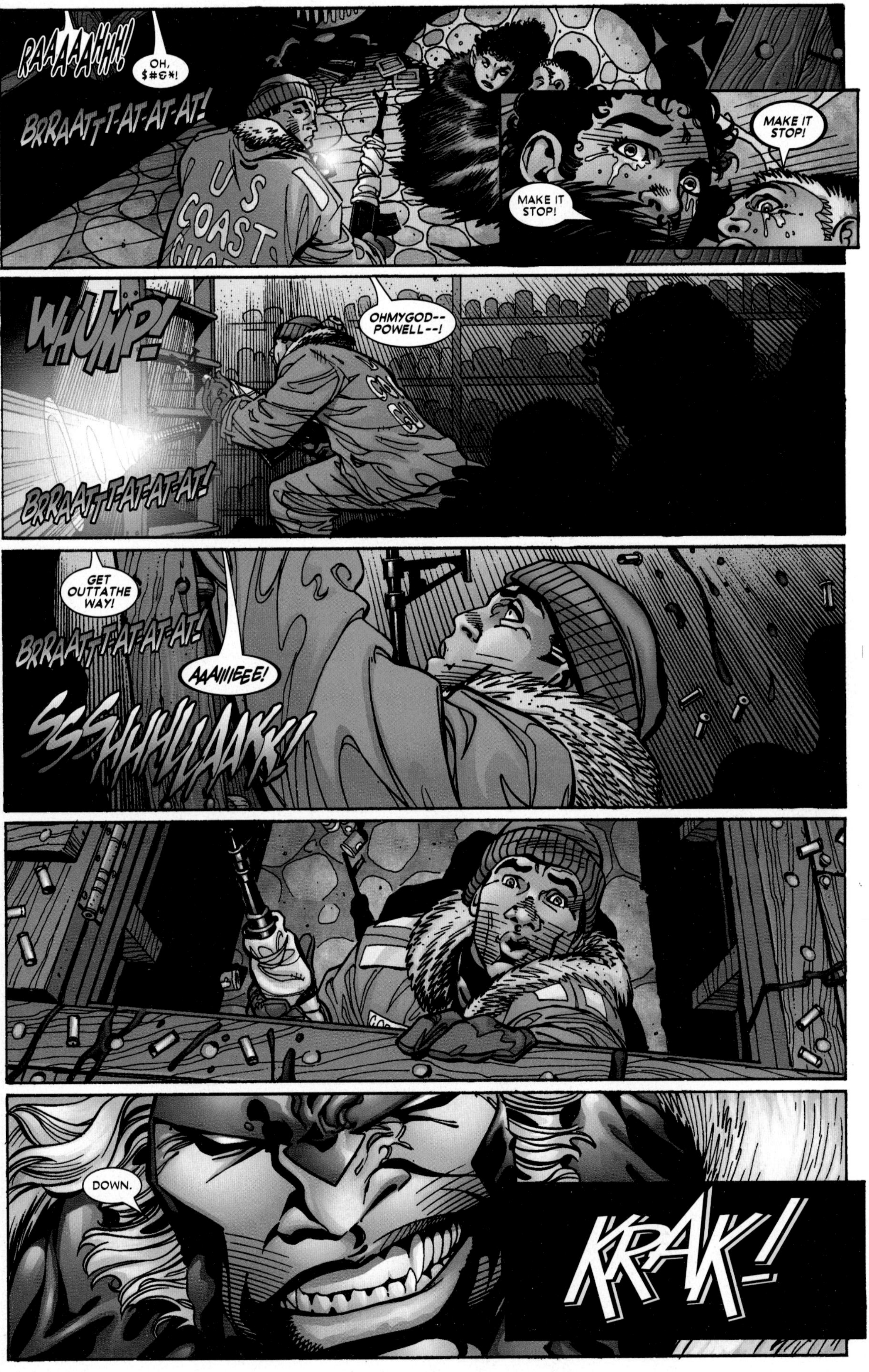
RAAAAAHHH!
OH, $#&*!
BRRAATT-T-AT-AT-AT!
MAKE IT STOP!
MAKE IT STOP!
WHUMP!
OHMYGOD-- POWELL--!
BRRAATT-T-AT-AT-AT!
GET OUTTATHE WAY!
BRRAATT-T-AT-AT-AT!
AAAIIIEEE!
SSSHHLLAAKK!
DOWN.
KRAK-!

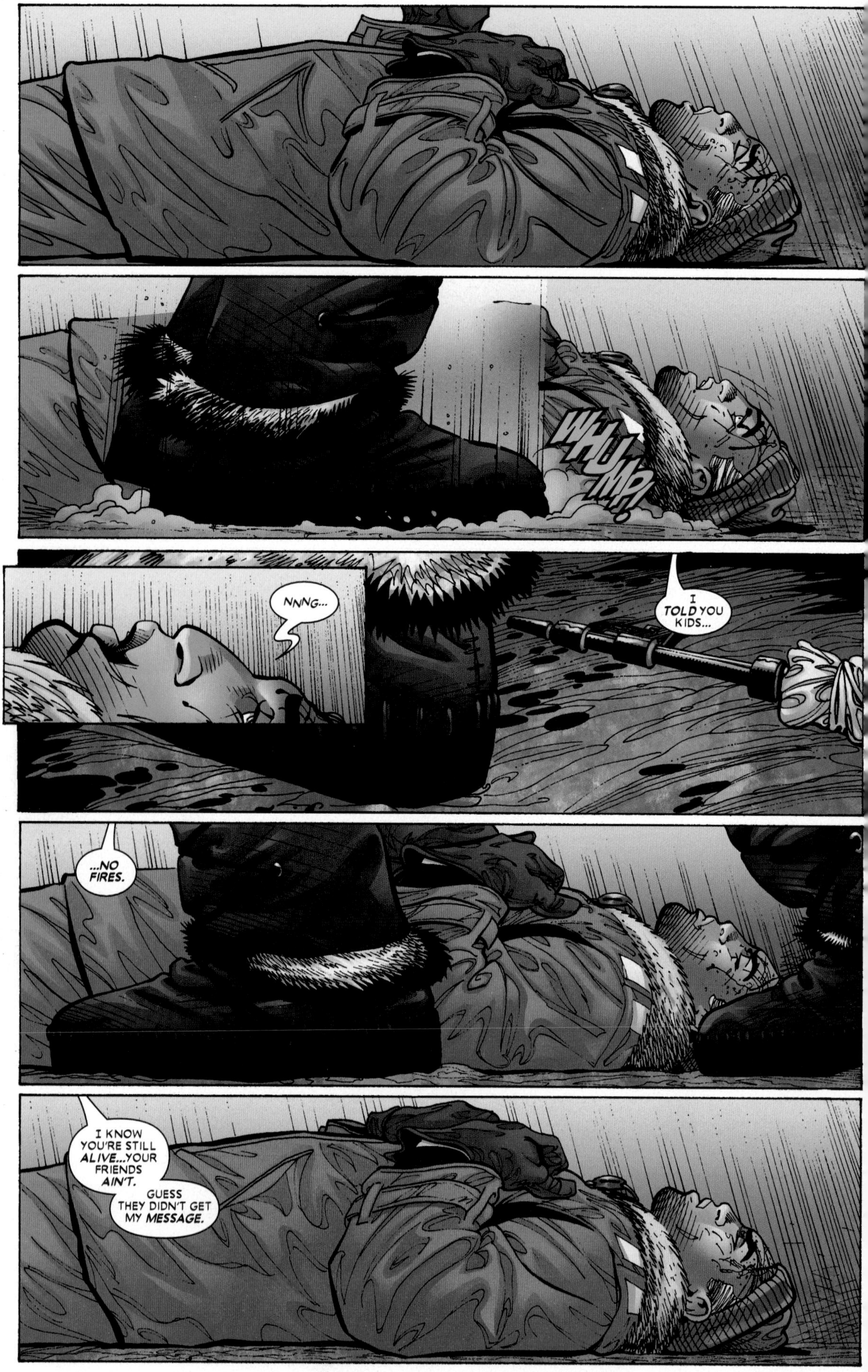
WHUMP!
NNNG...
I TOLD YOU KIDS...
...NO FIRES.
I KNOW YOU'RE STILL ALIVE...YOUR FRIENDS AIN'T.
GUESS THEY DIDN'T GET MY MESSAGE.

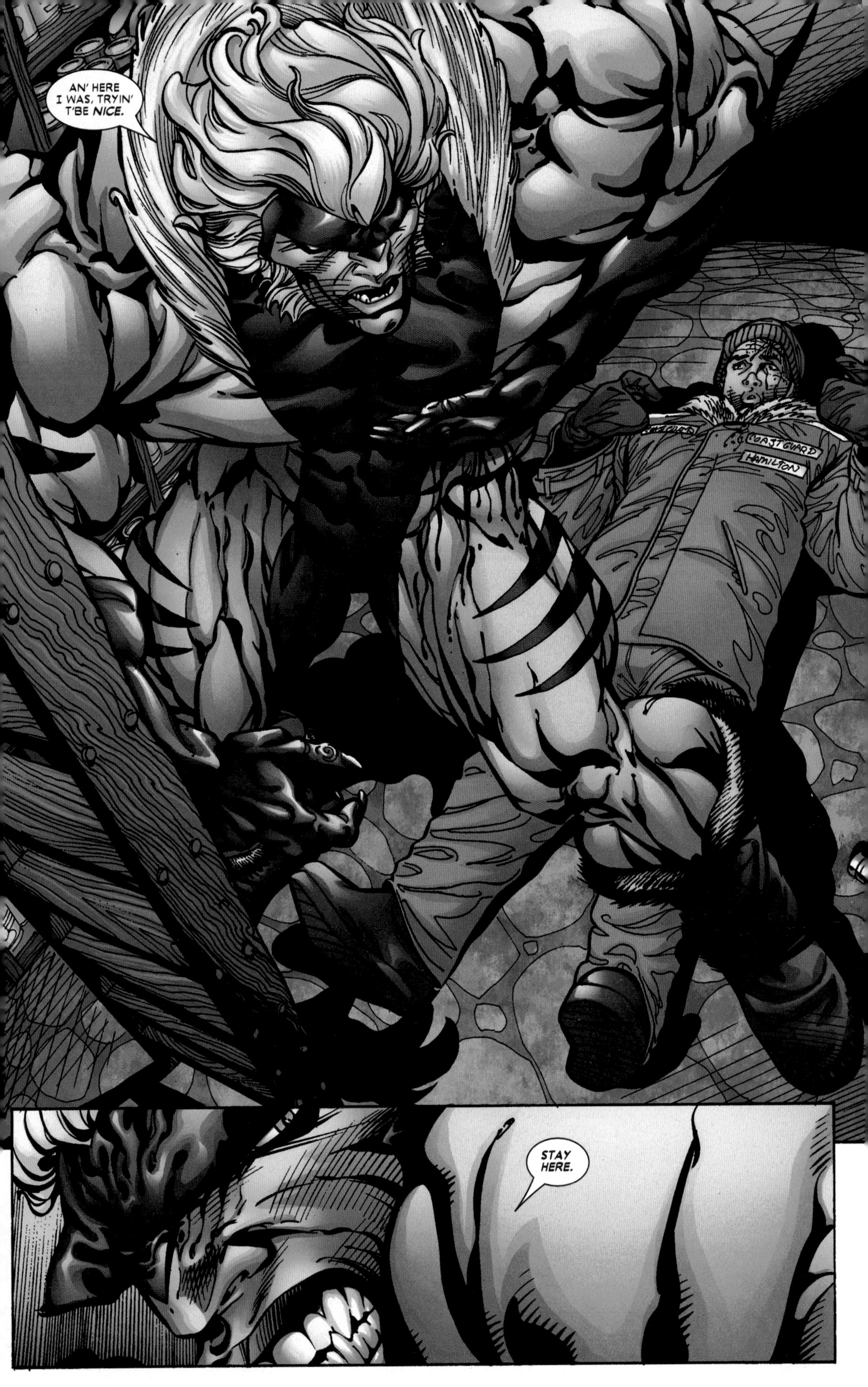
AN' HERE I WAS, TRYIN' T'BE *NICE.*
COAST GUARD
HAMILTON
STAY HERE.

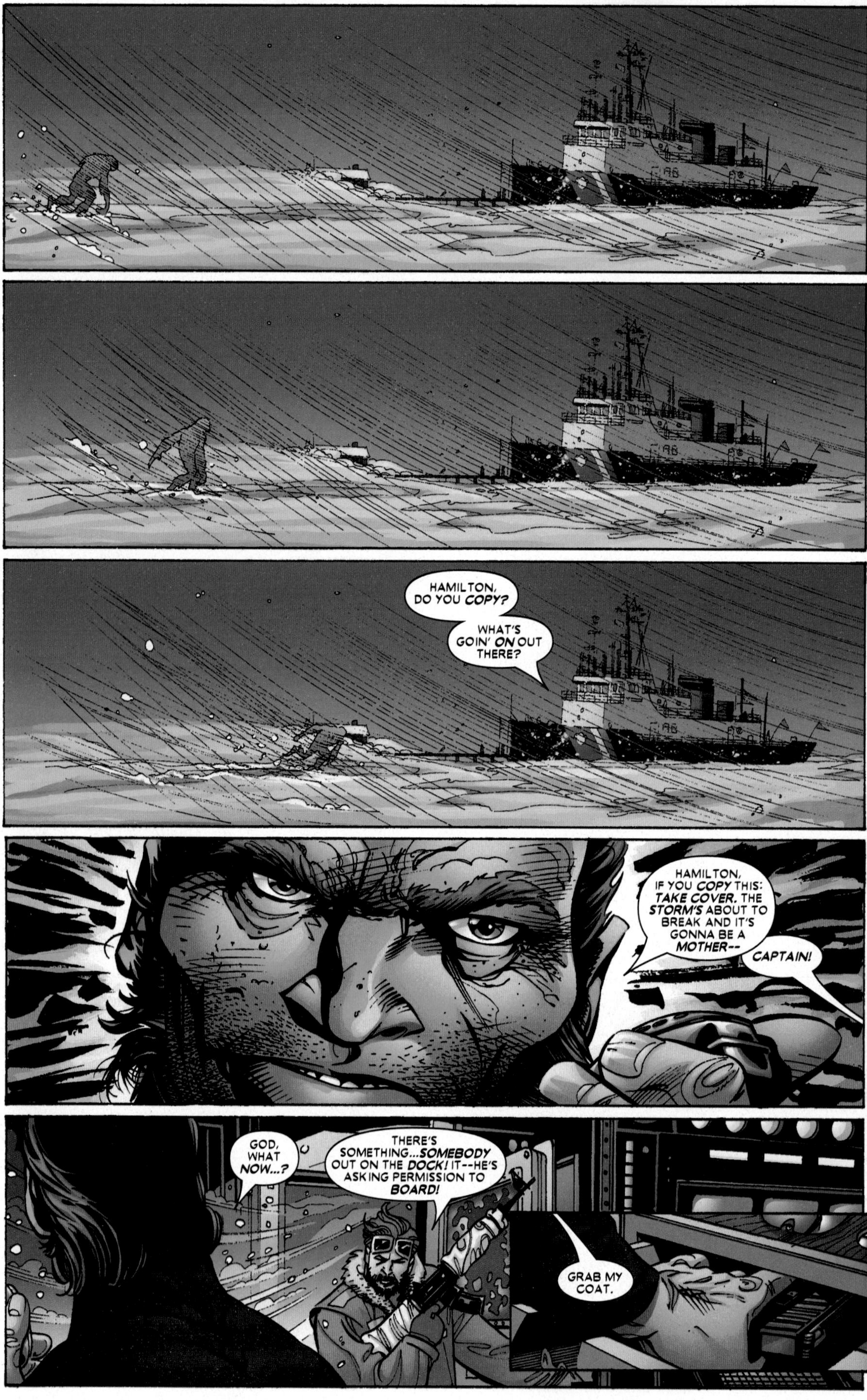
HAMILTON, DO YOU COPY?
WHAT'S GOIN' ON OUT THERE?
HAMILTON, IF YOU COPY THIS: TAKE COVER. THE STORM'S ABOUT TO BREAK AND IT'S GONNA BE A MOTHER--
CAPTAIN!
GOD, WHAT NOW...?
THERE'S SOMETHING...SOMEBODY OUT ON THE DOCK! IT--HE'S ASKING PERMISSION TO BOARD!
GRAB MY COAT.

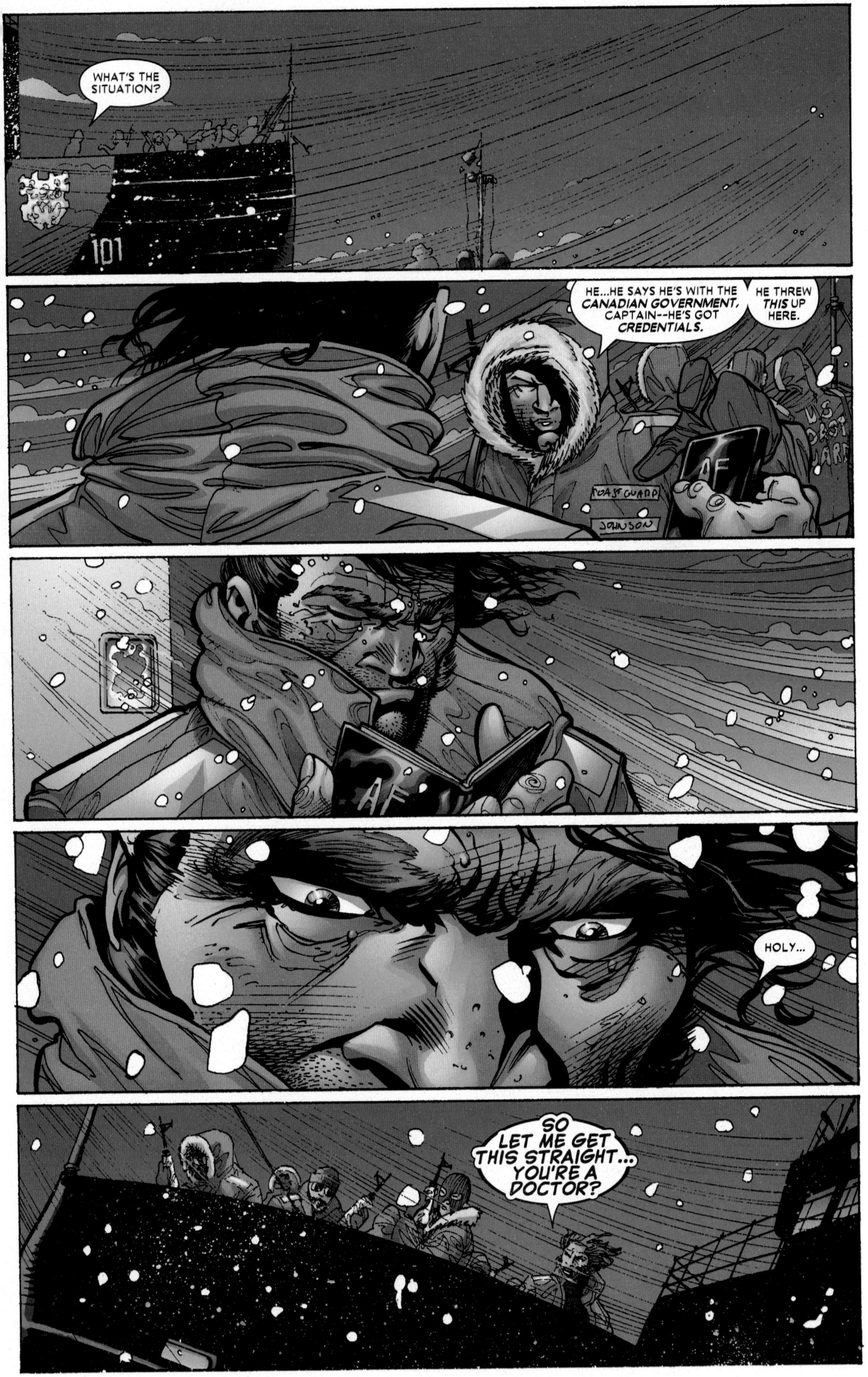
WHAT'S THE SITUATION?
101
HE...HE SAYS HE'S WITH THE *CANADIAN GOVERNMENT,* CAPTAIN--HE'S GOT *CREDENTIALS.*
HE THREW *THIS* UP HERE.
AF
JOHNSON
AF
HOLY...
SO LET ME GET THIS STRAIGHT... YOU'RE A DOCTOR?

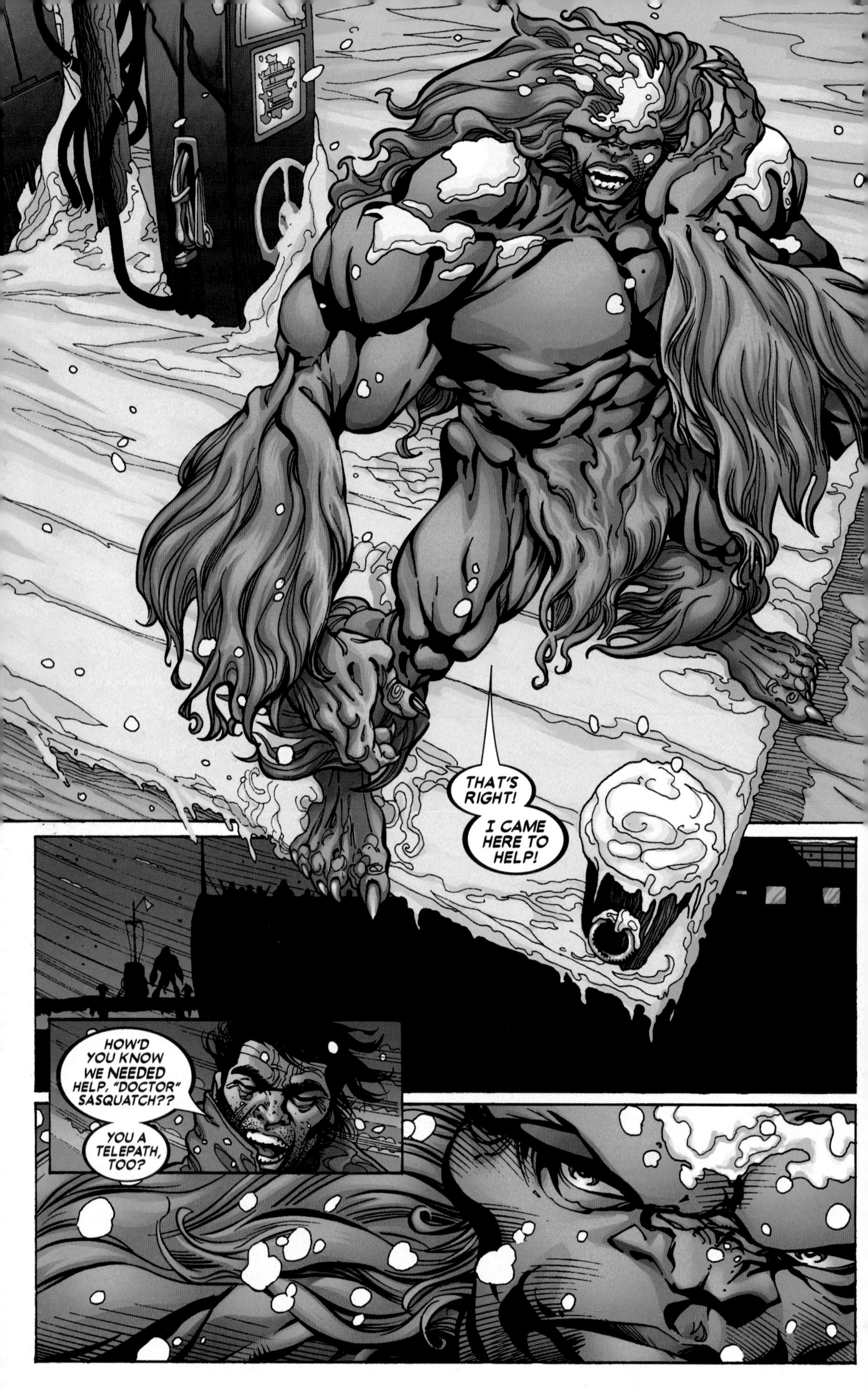
THAT'S RIGHT!
I CAME HERE TO HELP!
HOW'D YOU KNOW WE NEEDED HELP, "DOCTOR" SASQUATCH??
YOU A TELEPATH, TOO?

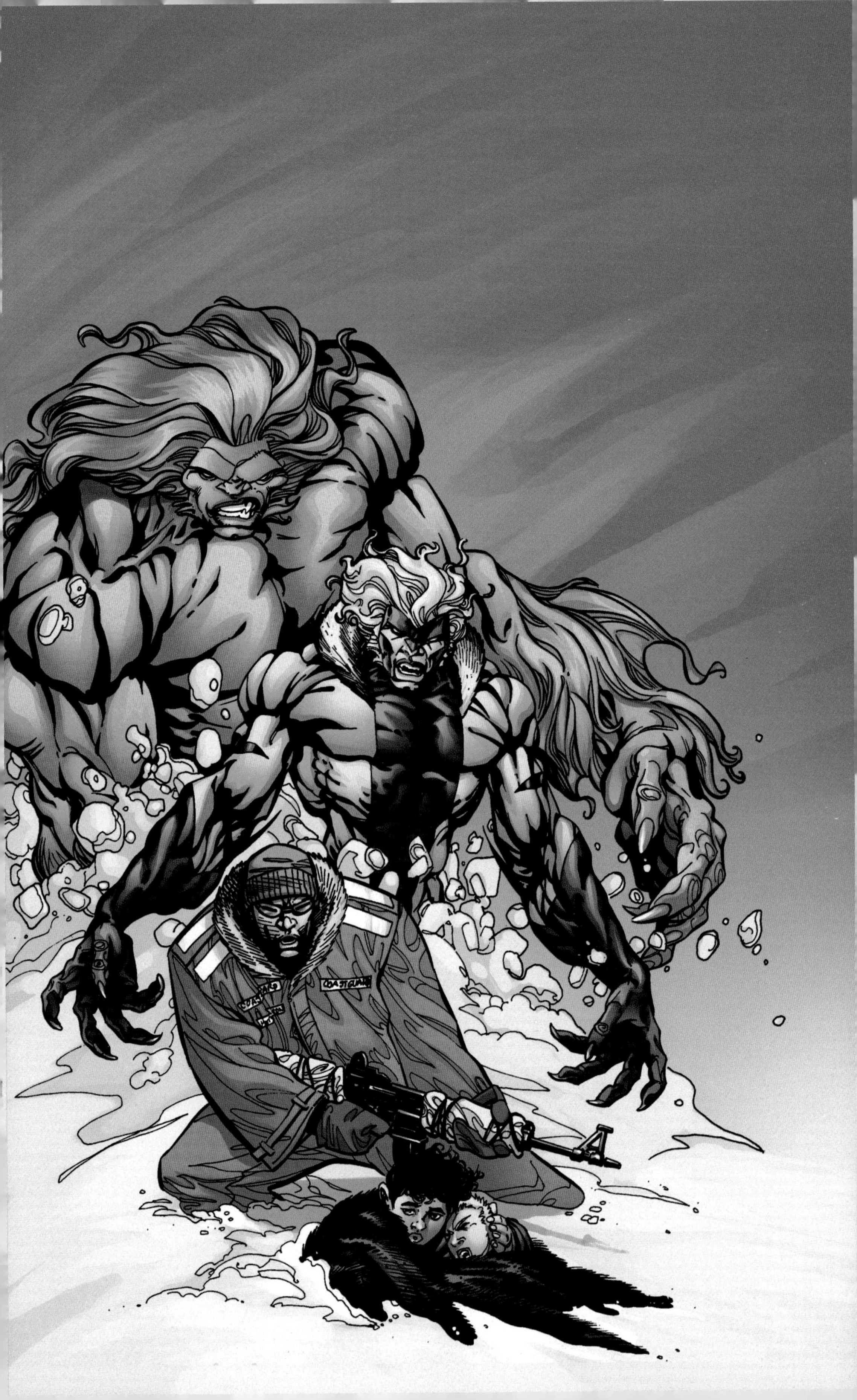

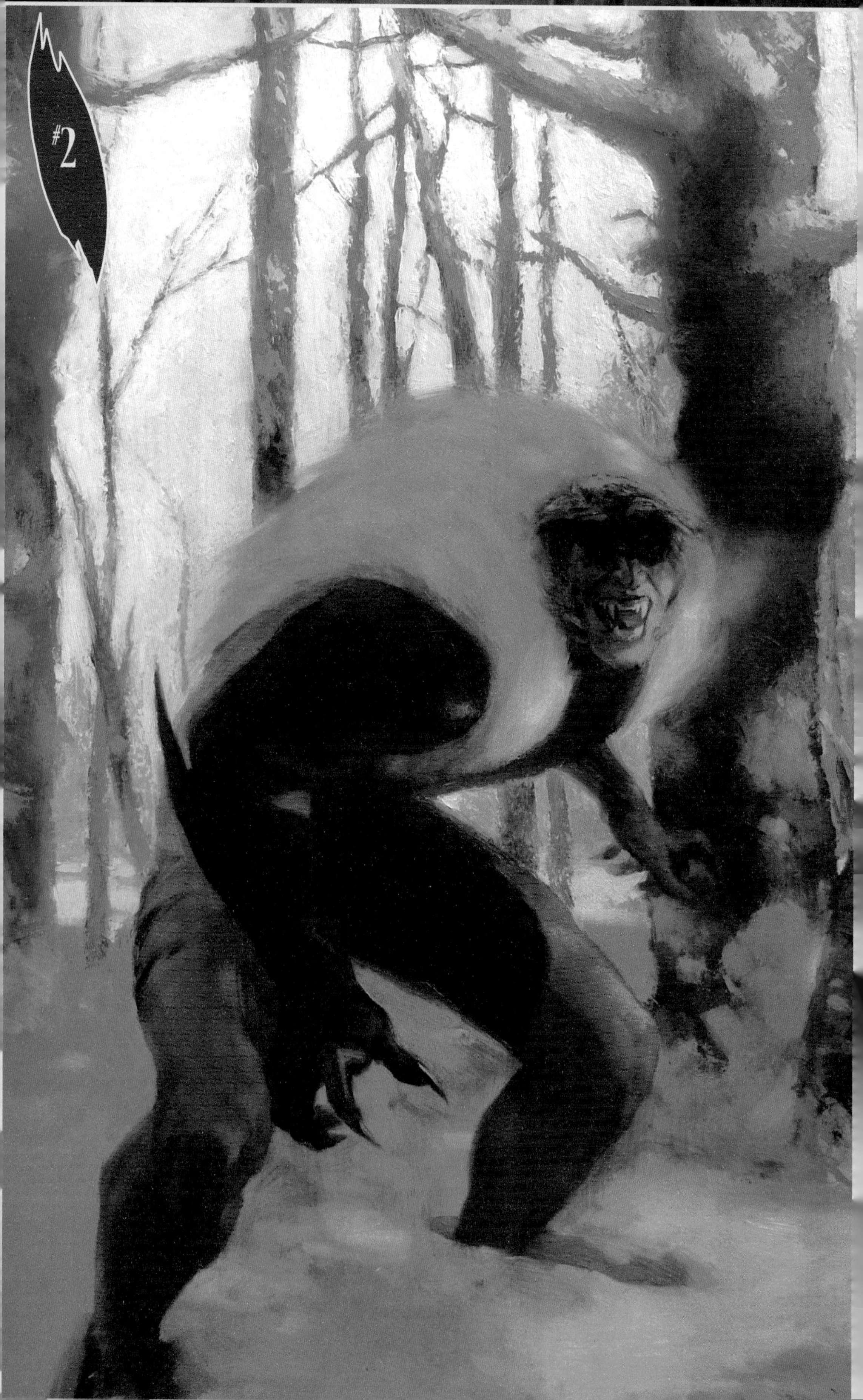
#2

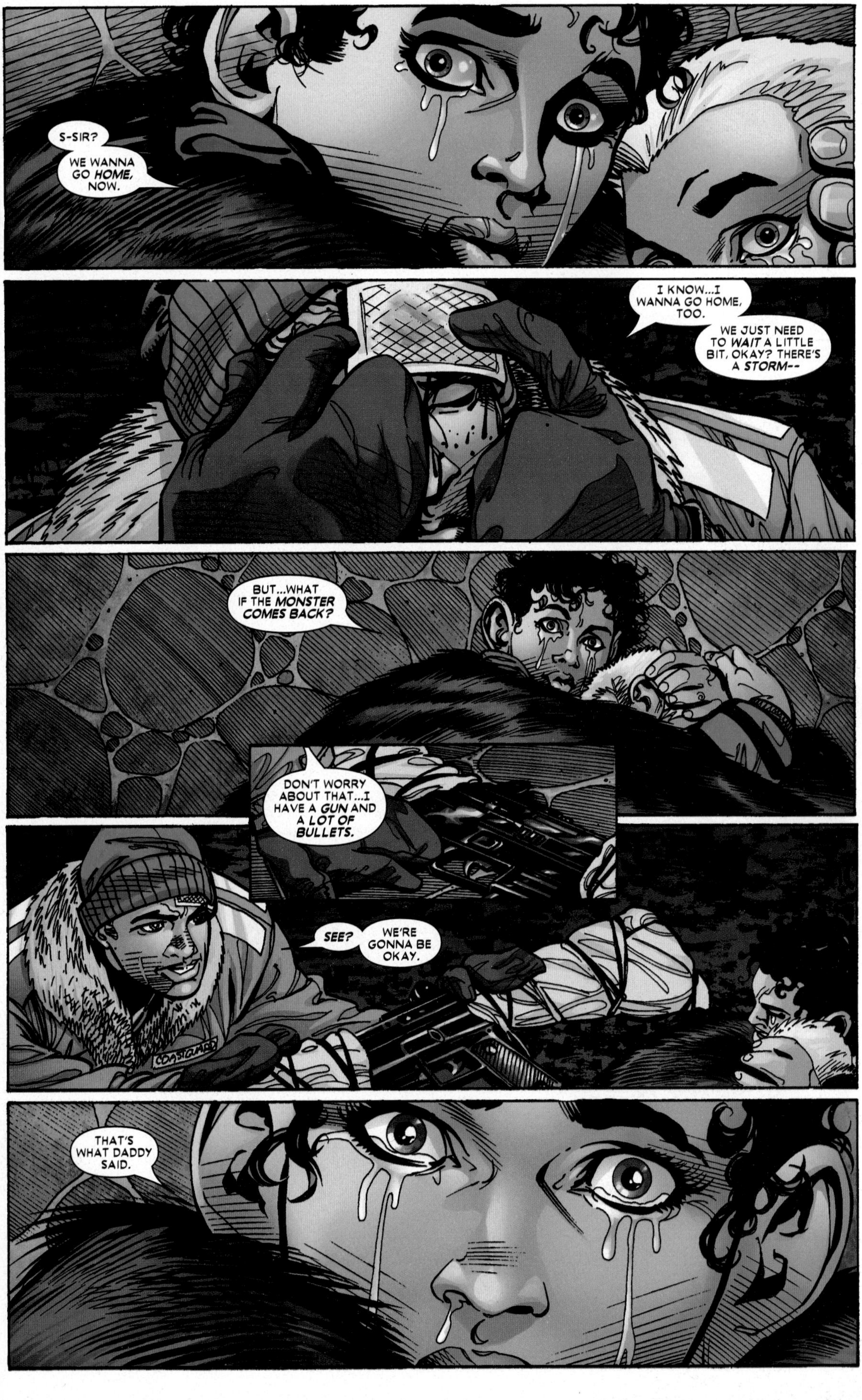
S-SIR?
WE WANNA GO *HOME,* NOW.
I KNOW...I WANNA GO HOME, TOO.
WE JUST NEED TO *WAIT* A LITTLE BIT, OKAY? THERE'S A *STORM--*
BUT...WHAT IF THE *MONSTER COMES BACK?*
DON'T WORRY ABOUT THAT...I HAVE A *GUN* AND A *LOT OF BULLETS.*
SEE?
WE'RE GONNA BE OKAY.
COASTGUARD
THAT'S WHAT DADDY SAID.

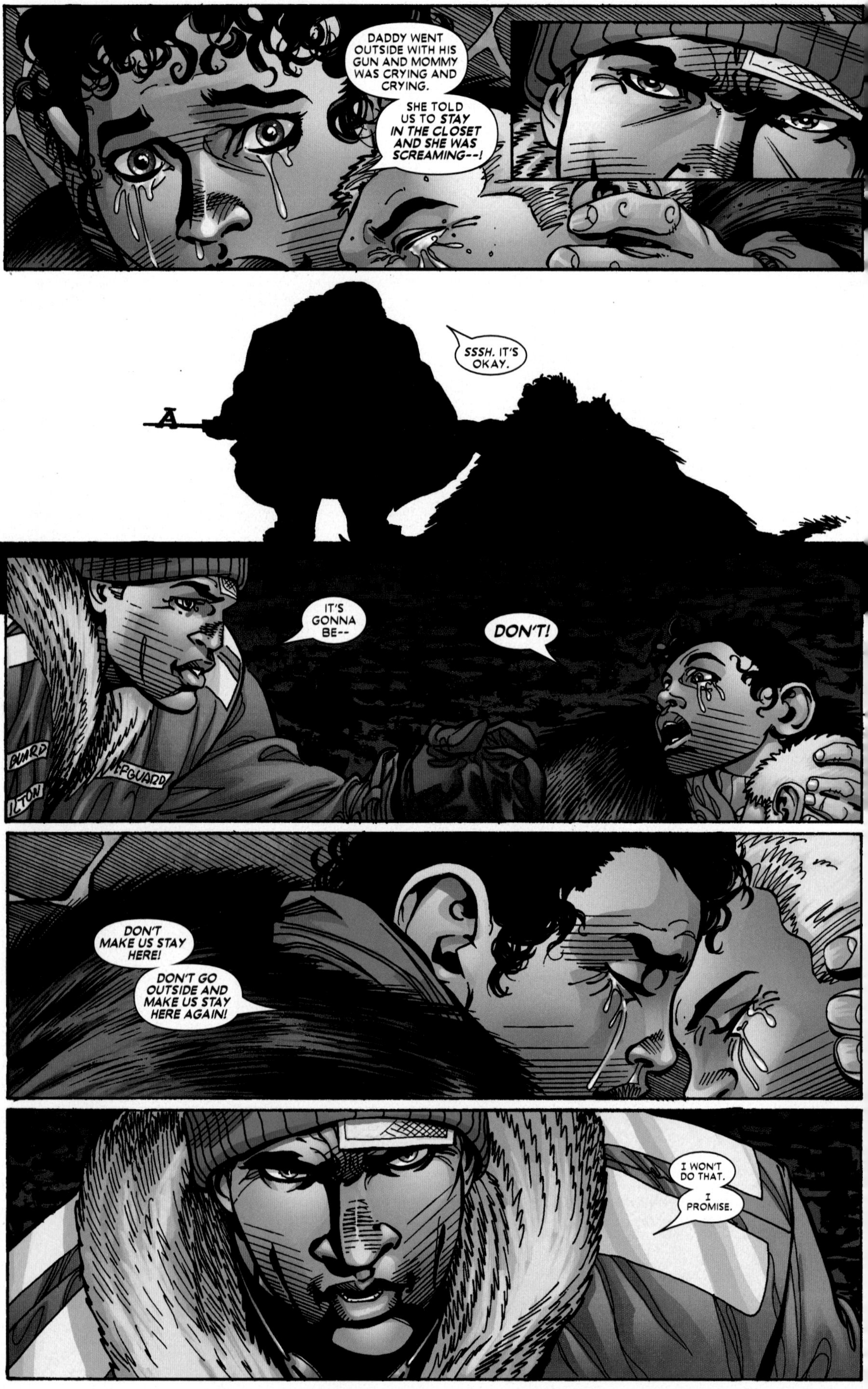
DADDY WENT OUTSIDE WITH HIS GUN AND MOMMY WAS CRYING AND CRYING.
SHE TOLD US TO *STAY IN THE CLOSET AND SHE WAS SCREAMING--!*
SSSH. IT'S OKAY.
IT'S GONNA BE--
DON'T!
DON'T MAKE US STAY HERE!
DON'T GO OUTSIDE AND MAKE US STAY HERE AGAIN!
I WON'T DO THAT.
I PROMISE.

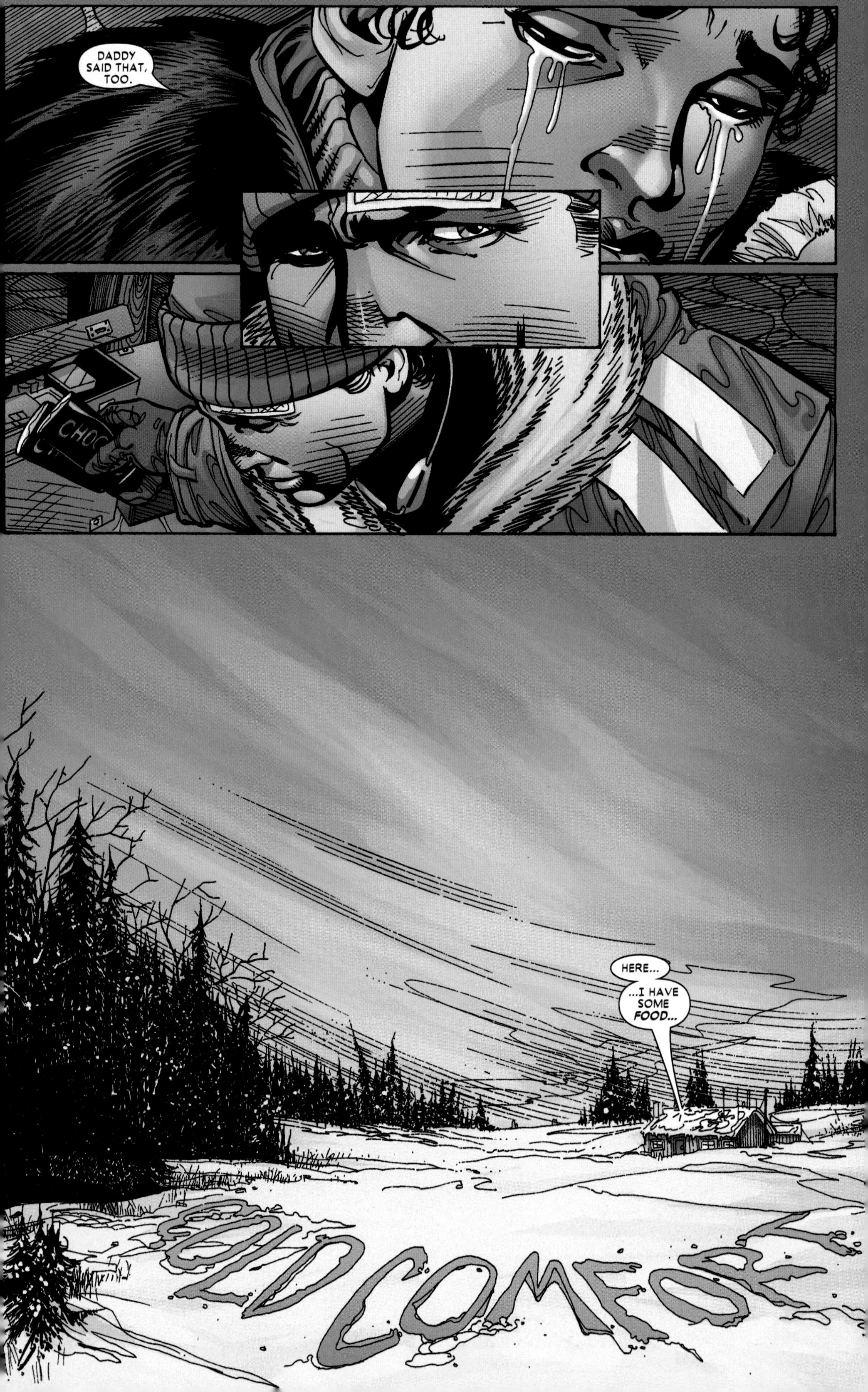
DADDY SAID THAT, TOO.
HERE...
...I HAVE SOME FOOD...

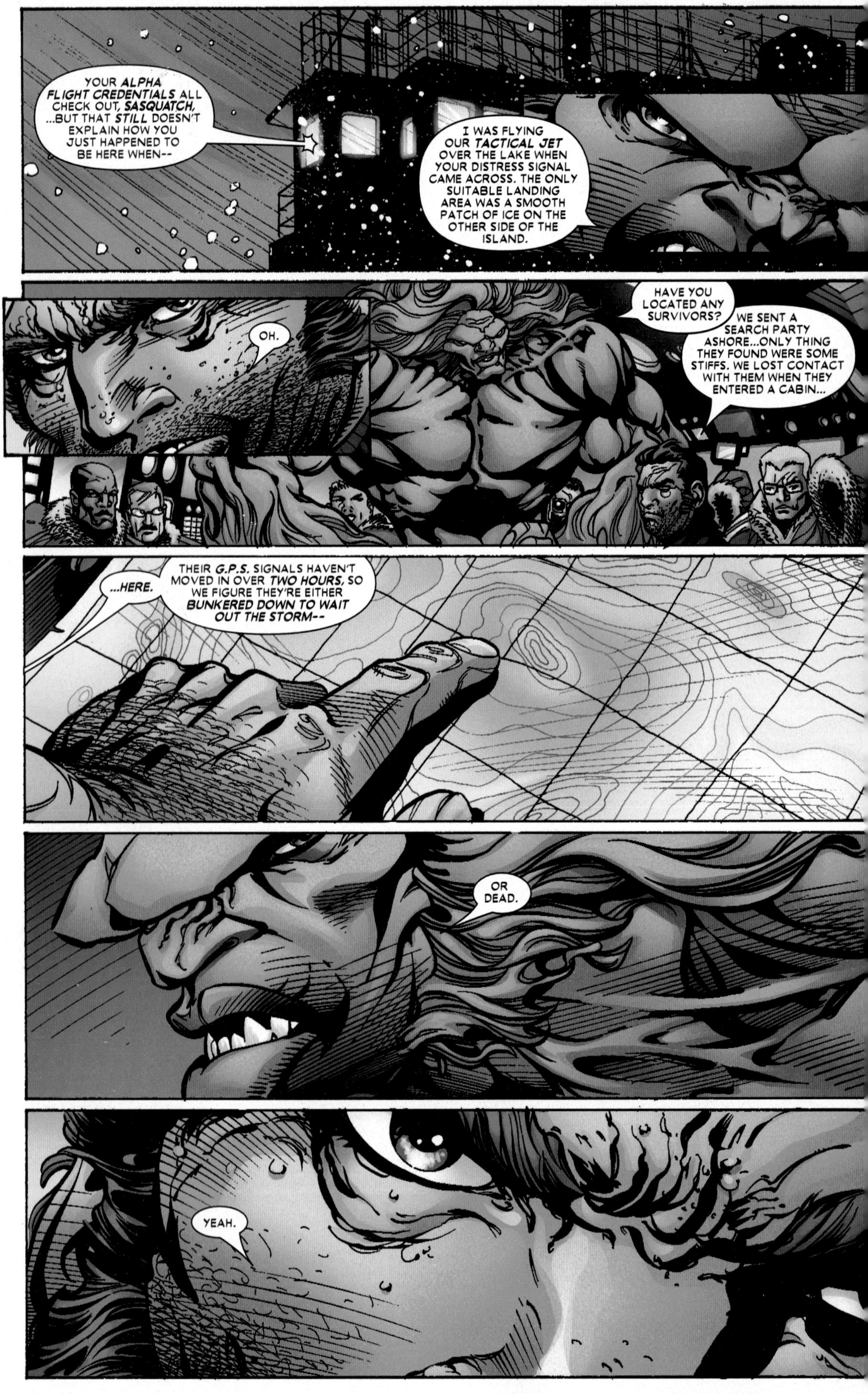
YOUR ALPHA FLIGHT CREDENTIALS ALL CHECK OUT, SASQUATCH, ...BUT THAT STILL DOESN'T EXPLAIN HOW YOU JUST HAPPENED TO BE HERE WHEN--
I WAS FLYING OUR TACTICAL JET OVER THE LAKE WHEN YOUR DISTRESS SIGNAL CAME ACROSS. THE ONLY SUITABLE LANDING AREA WAS A SMOOTH PATCH OF ICE ON THE OTHER SIDE OF THE ISLAND.
OH.
HAVE YOU LOCATED ANY SURVIVORS?
WE SENT A SEARCH PARTY ASHORE...ONLY THING THEY FOUND WERE SOME STIFFS. WE LOST CONTACT WITH THEM WHEN THEY ENTERED A CABIN...
...HERE.
THEIR G.P.S. SIGNALS HAVEN'T MOVED IN OVER TWO HOURS, SO WE FIGURE THEY'RE EITHER BUNKERED DOWN TO WAIT OUT THE STORM--
OR DEAD.
YEAH.

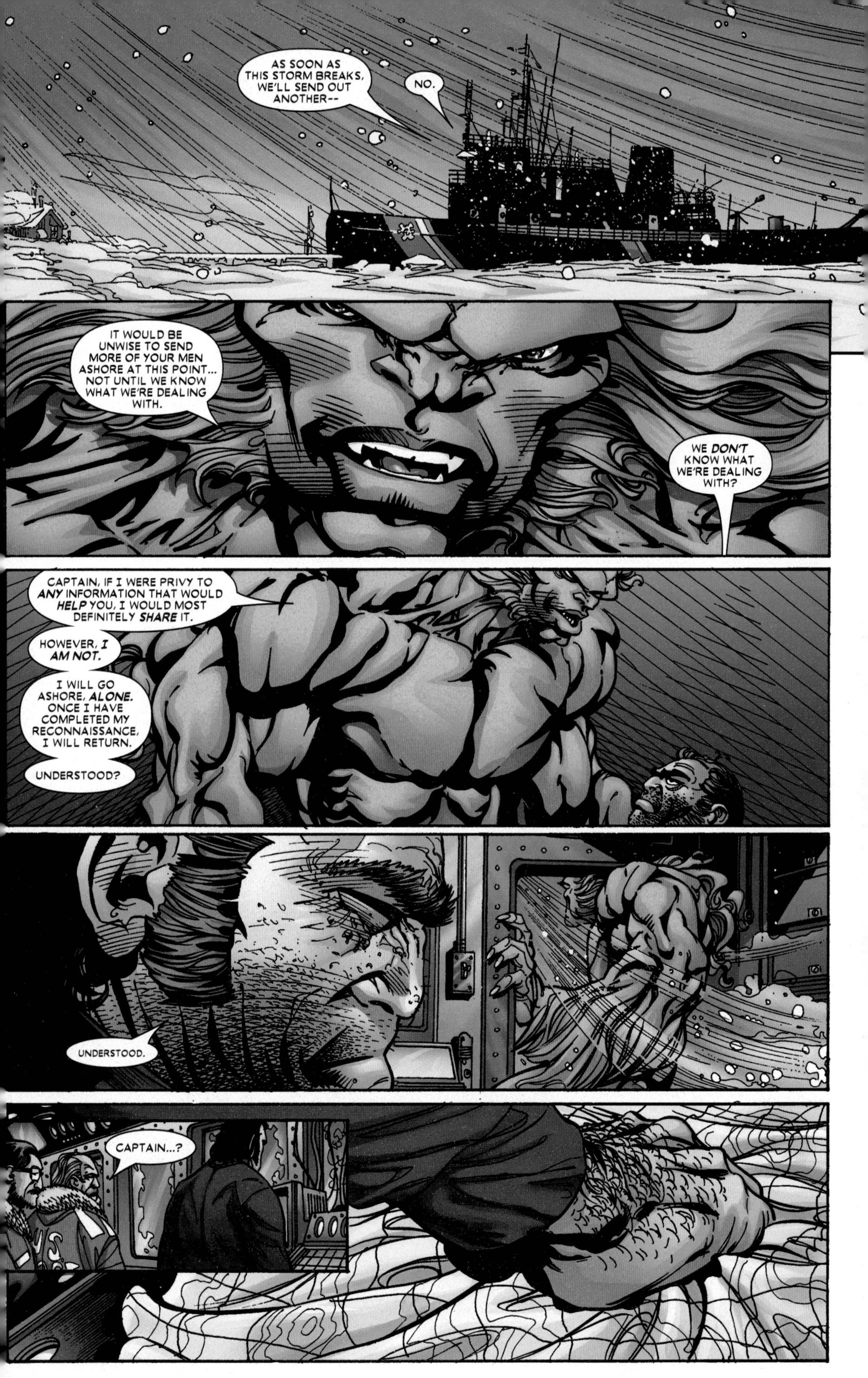
AS SOON AS THIS STORM BREAKS, WE'LL SEND OUT ANOTHER--
NO.
IT WOULD BE UNWISE TO SEND MORE OF YOUR MEN ASHORE AT THIS POINT... NOT UNTIL WE KNOW WHAT WE'RE DEALING WITH.
WE *DON'T* KNOW WHAT WE'RE DEALING WITH?
CAPTAIN, IF I WERE PRIVY TO *ANY* INFORMATION THAT WOULD *HELP* YOU, I WOULD MOST DEFINITELY *SHARE* IT.
HOWEVER, *I AM NOT.*
I WILL GO ASHORE, *ALONE.* ONCE I HAVE COMPLETED MY RECONNAISSANCE, I WILL RETURN.
UNDERSTOOD?
UNDERSTOOD.
CAPTAIN...?

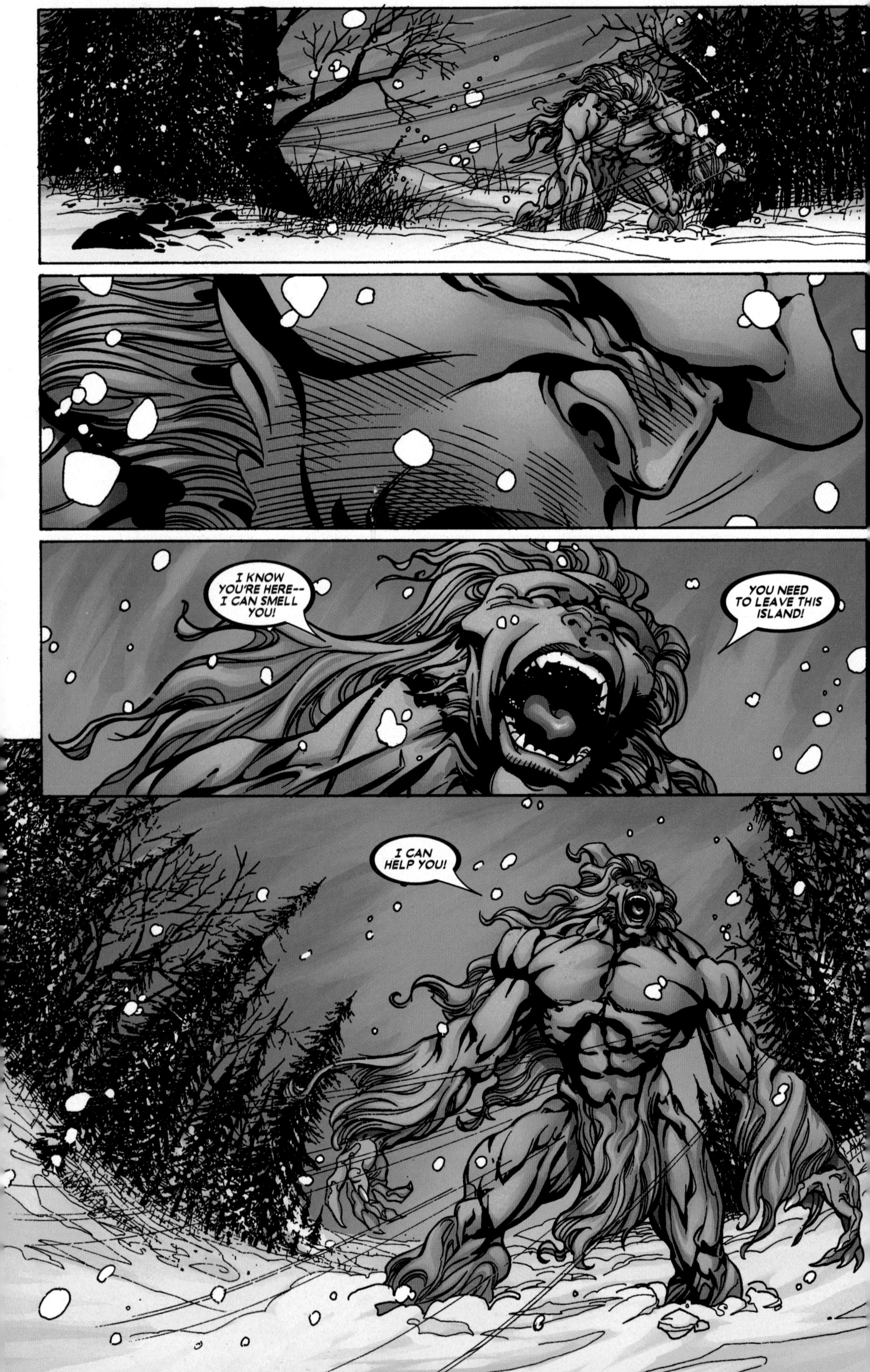
I KNOW YOU'RE HERE-- I CAN SMELL YOU!
YOU NEED TO LEAVE THIS ISLAND!
I CAN HELP YOU!

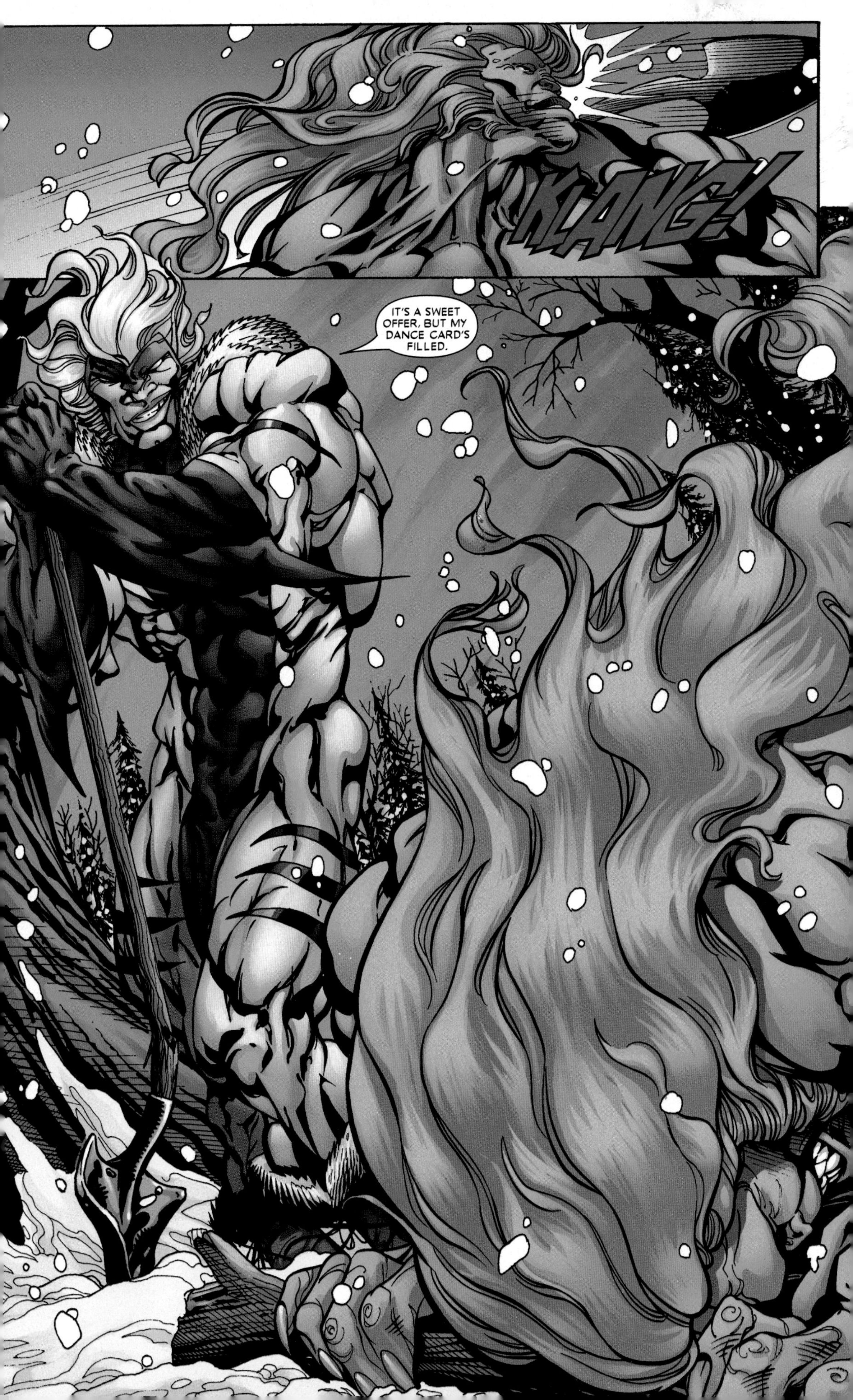
KLANG!
IT'S A SWEET OFFER, BUT MY DANCE CARD'S FILLED.

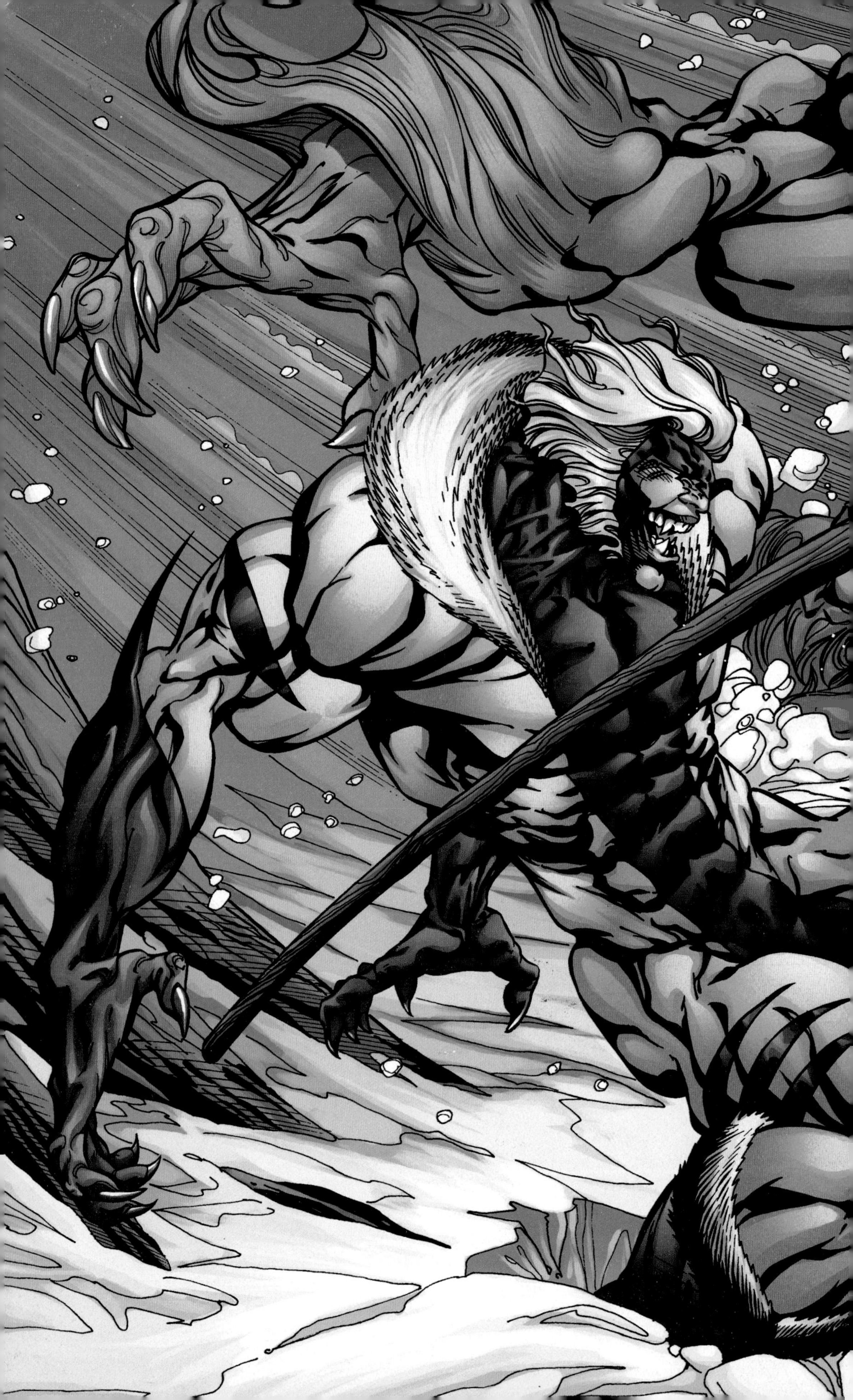

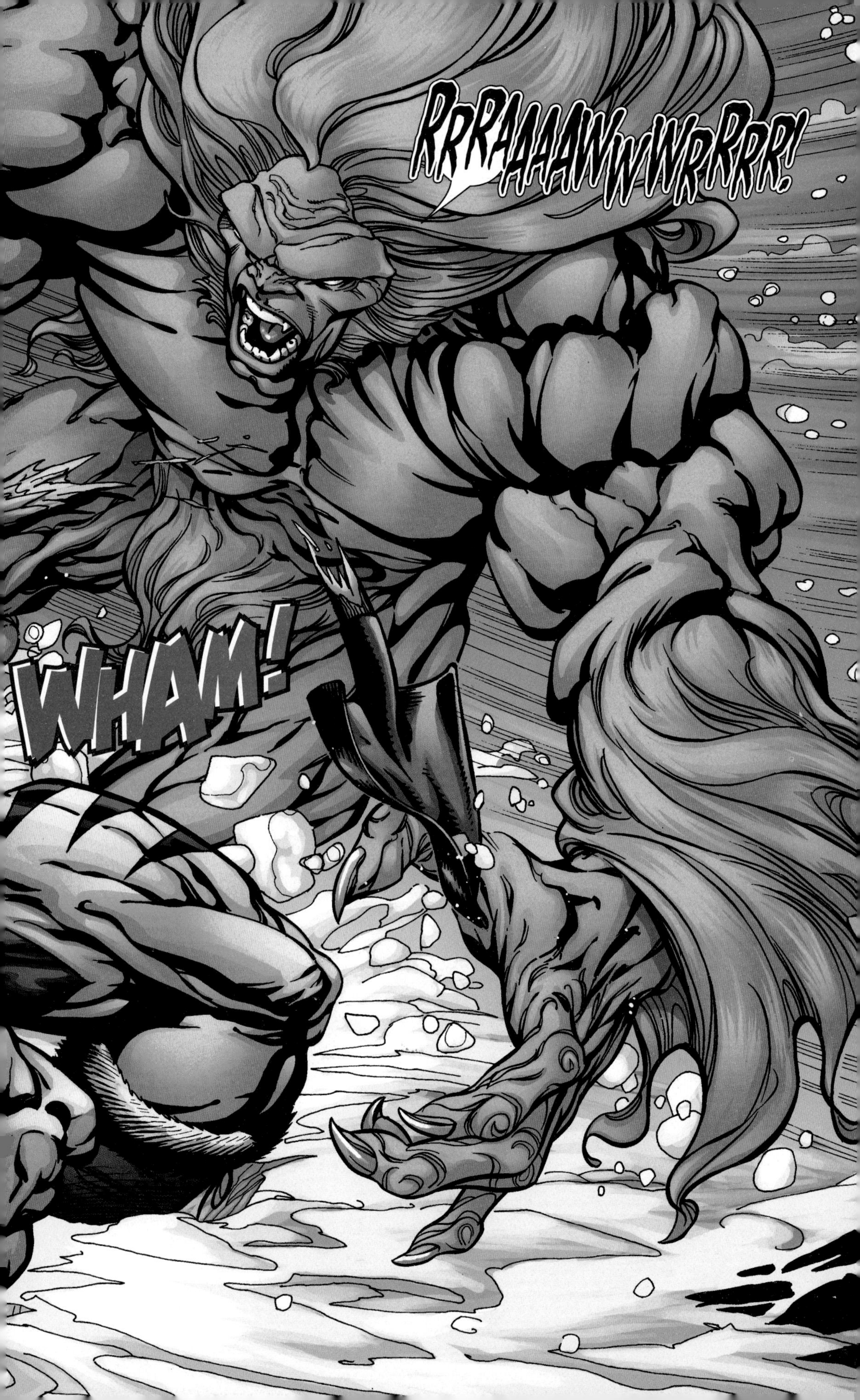
RRRAAAAWWRRRR!
WHAM!

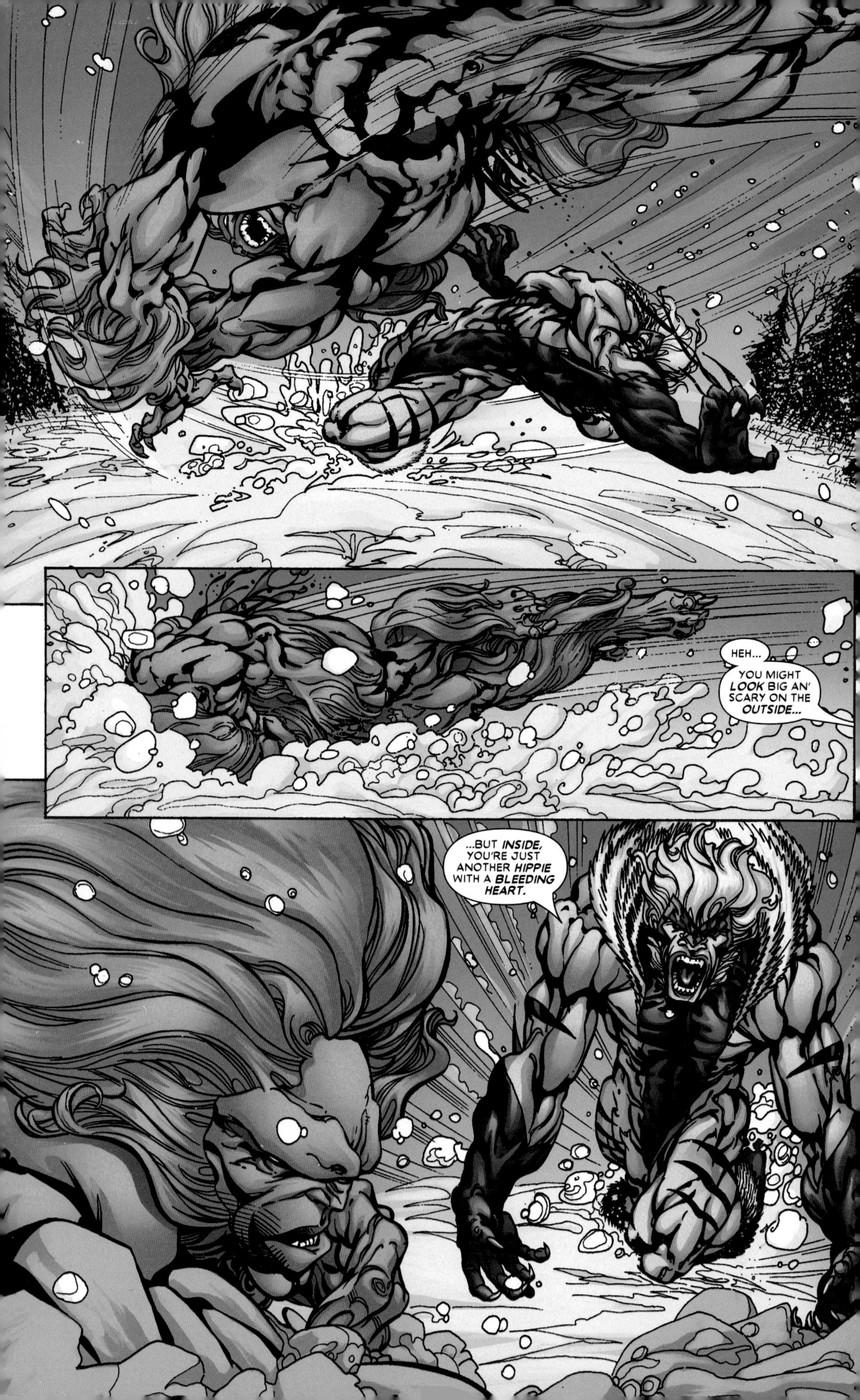
HEH...
YOU MIGHT *LOOK* BIG AN' SCARY ON THE *OUTSIDE*...
...BUT *INSIDE,* YOU'RE JUST ANOTHER *HIPPIE* WITH A *BLEEDING HEART.*

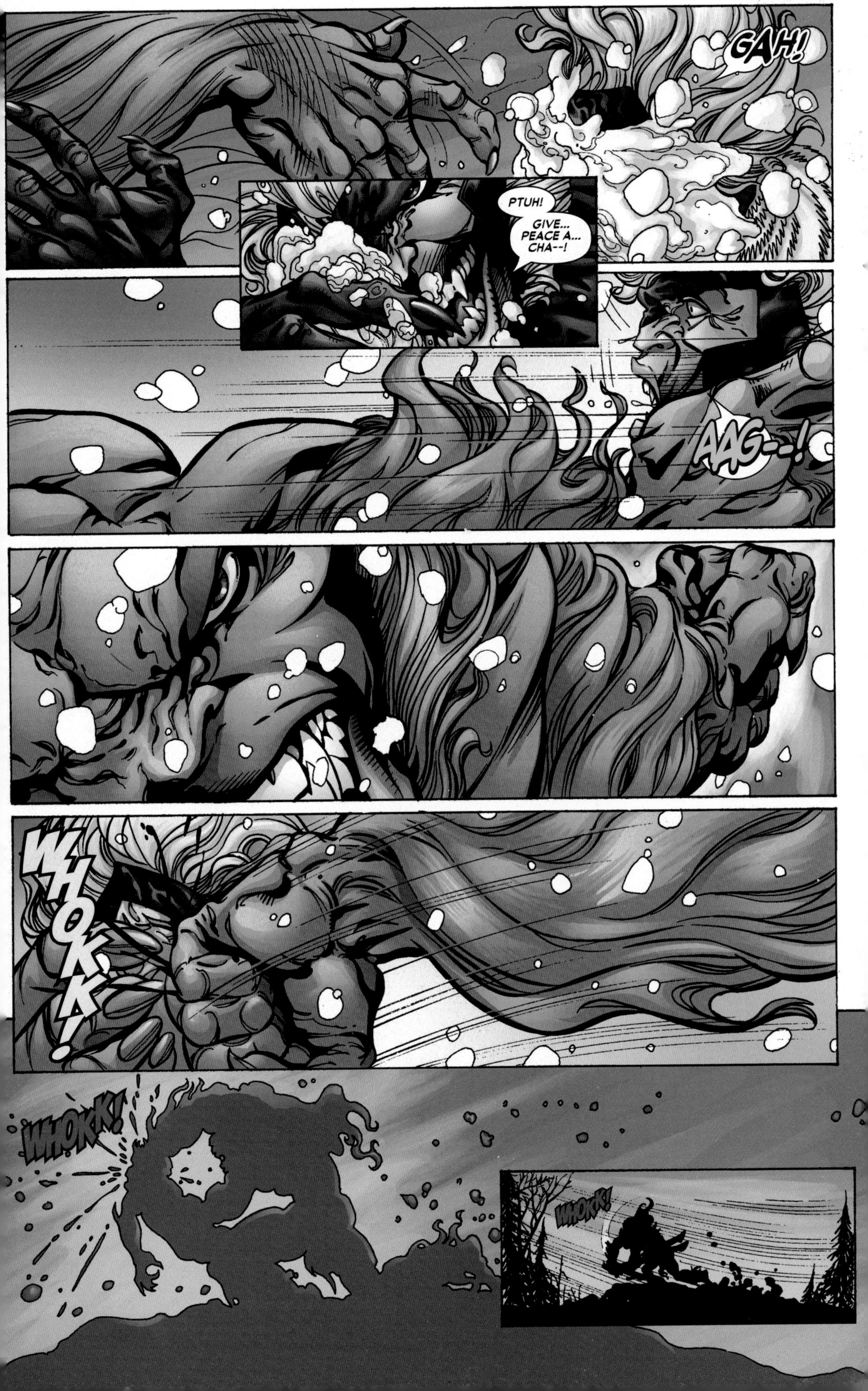
GAH!
PTUH!
GIVE... PEACE A... CHA--!
AAG--!
WHOKK!
WHOKK!
WHOKK!

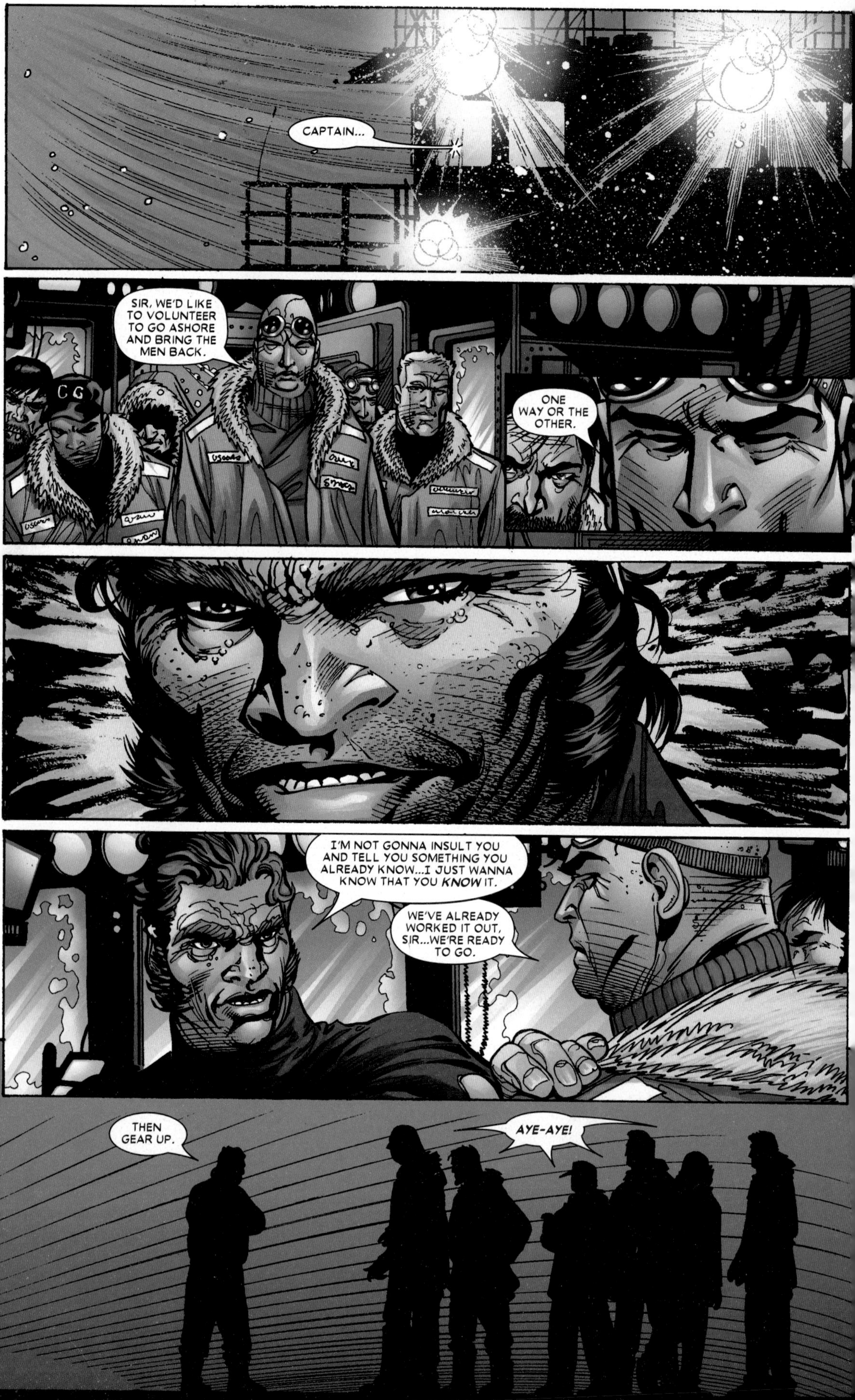
CAPTAIN...
SIR, WE'D LIKE TO VOLUNTEER TO GO ASHORE AND BRING THE MEN BACK.
ONE WAY OR THE OTHER.
I'M NOT GONNA INSULT YOU AND TELL YOU SOMETHING YOU ALREADY KNOW...I JUST WANNA KNOW THAT YOU *KNOW* IT.
WE'VE ALREADY WORKED IT OUT, SIR...WE'RE READY TO GO.
THEN GEAR UP.
AYE-AYE!

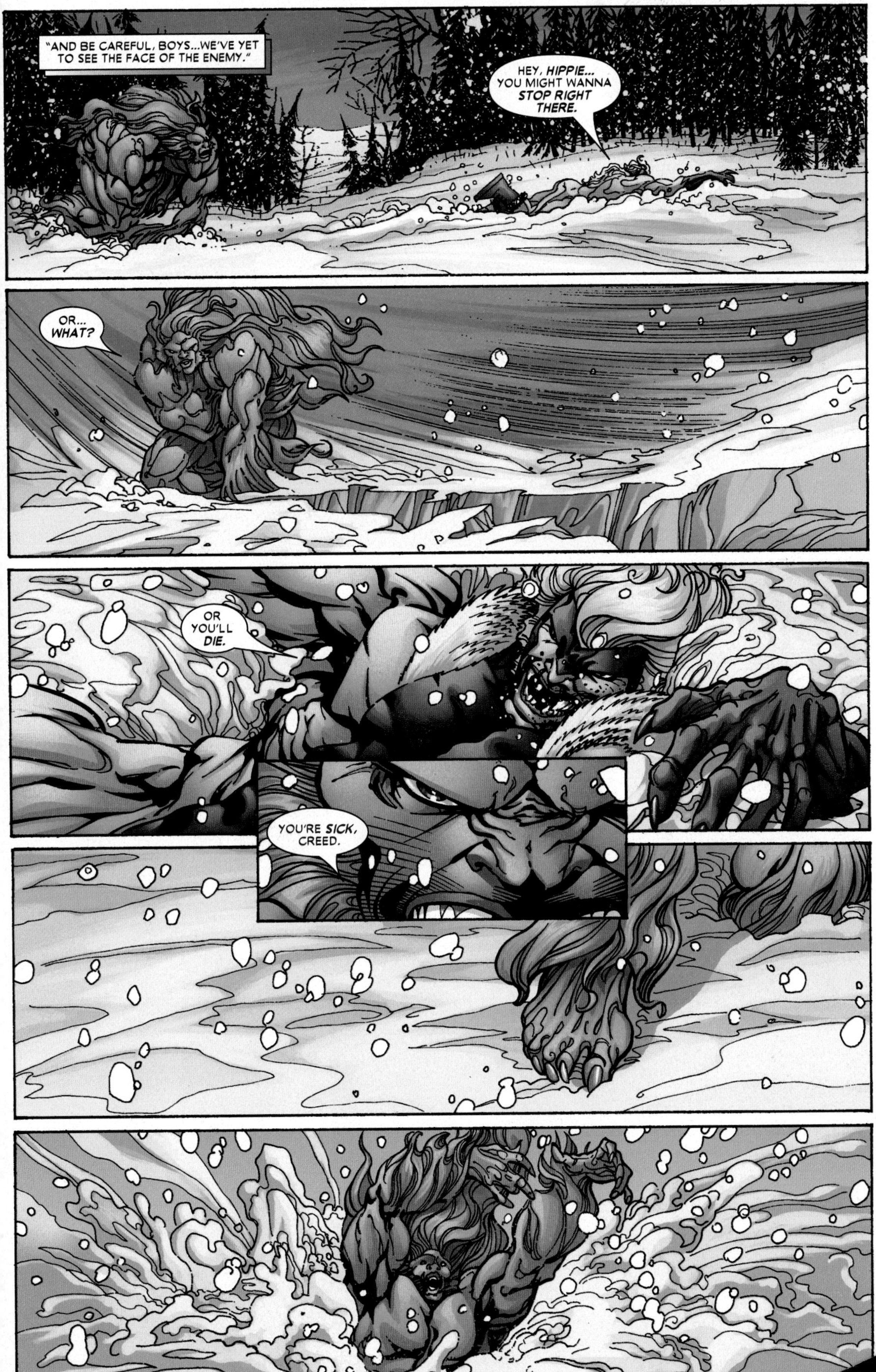
"AND BE CAREFUL, BOYS...WE'VE YET TO SEE THE FACE OF THE ENEMY."
HEY, HIPPIE... YOU MIGHT WANNA STOP RIGHT THERE.
OR... WHAT?
OR YOU'LL DIE.
YOU'RE SICK, CREED.

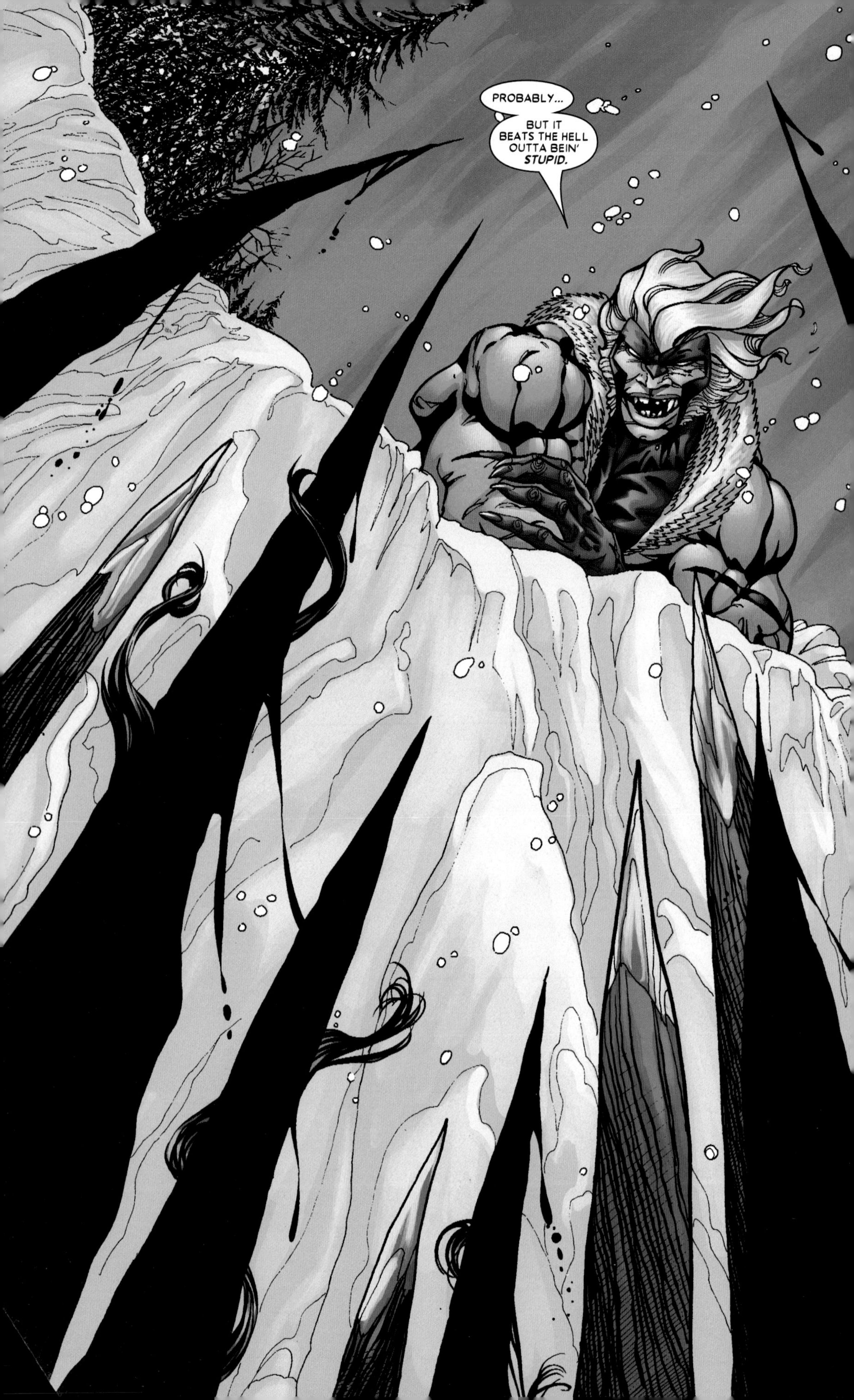
PROBABLY...
BUT IT BEATS THE HELL OUTTA BEIN' *STUPID.*

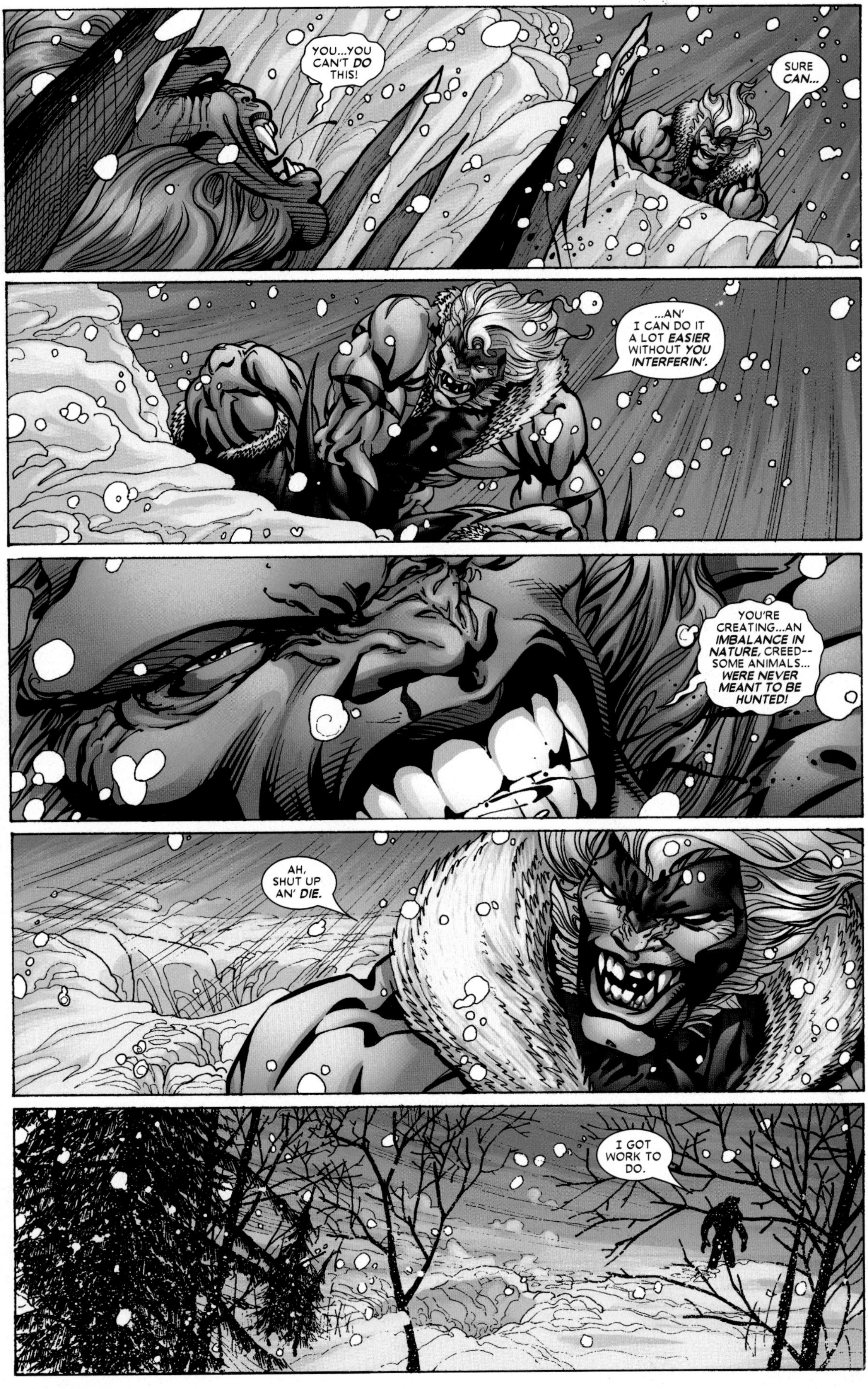
YOU...YOU CAN'T DO THIS!
SURE CAN...
...AN' I CAN DO IT A LOT EASIER WITHOUT YOU INTERFERIN'.
YOU'RE CREATING...AN IMBALANCE IN NATURE, CREED-- SOME ANIMALS... WERE NEVER MEANT TO BE HUNTED!
AH, SHUT UP AN' DIE.
I GOT WORK TO DO.

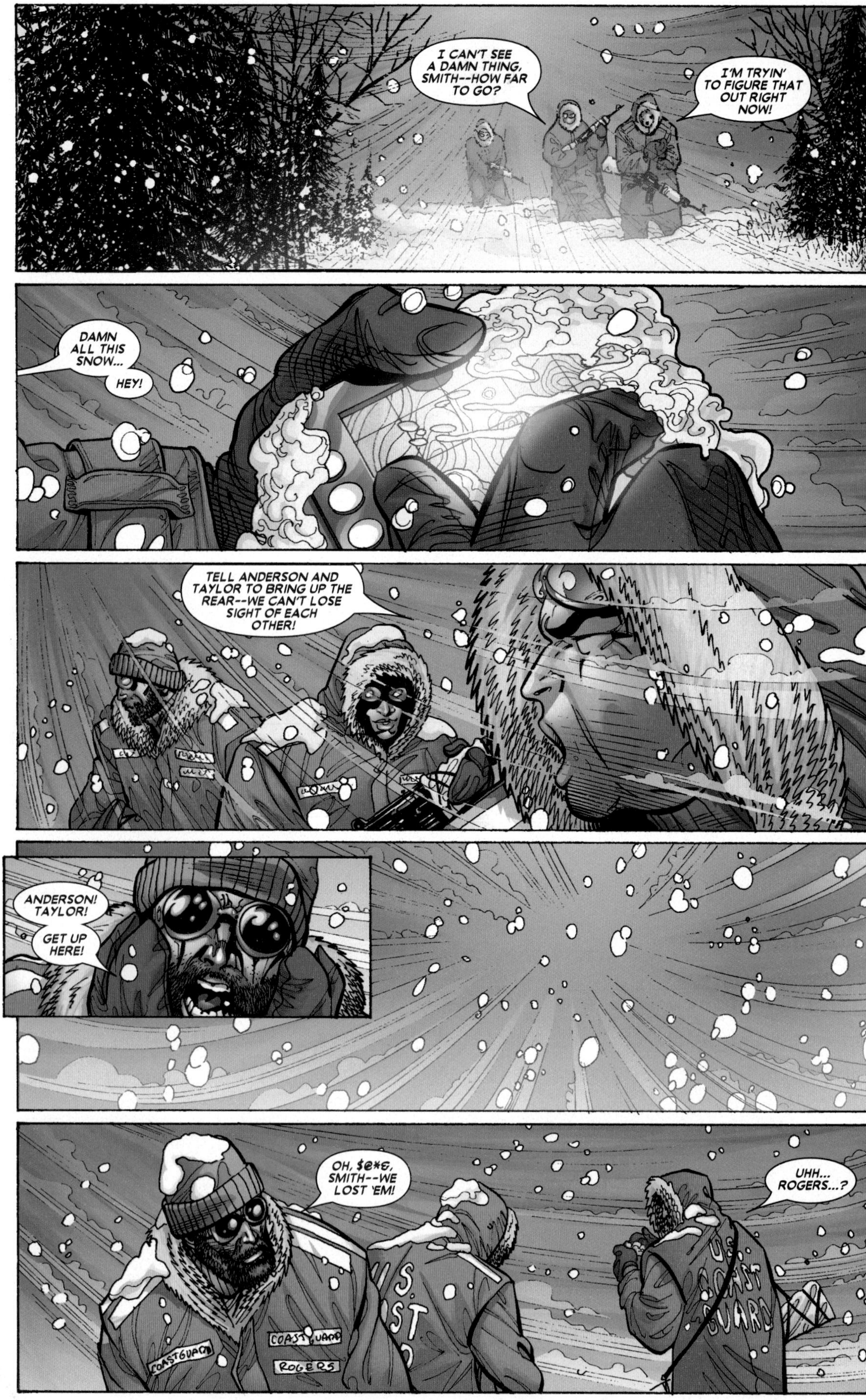
I CAN'T SEE A DAMN THING, SMITH--HOW FAR TO GO?
I'M TRYIN' TO FIGURE THAT OUT RIGHT NOW!
DAMN ALL THIS SNOW...
HEY!
TELL ANDERSON AND TAYLOR TO BRING UP THE REAR--WE CAN'T LOSE SIGHT OF EACH OTHER!
ANDERSON! TAYLOR!
GET UP HERE!
OH, $@*&, SMITH--WE LOST 'EM!
UHH... ROGERS...?
COASTGUARD
COASTGUARD
ROGERS
U.S. COAST GUARD

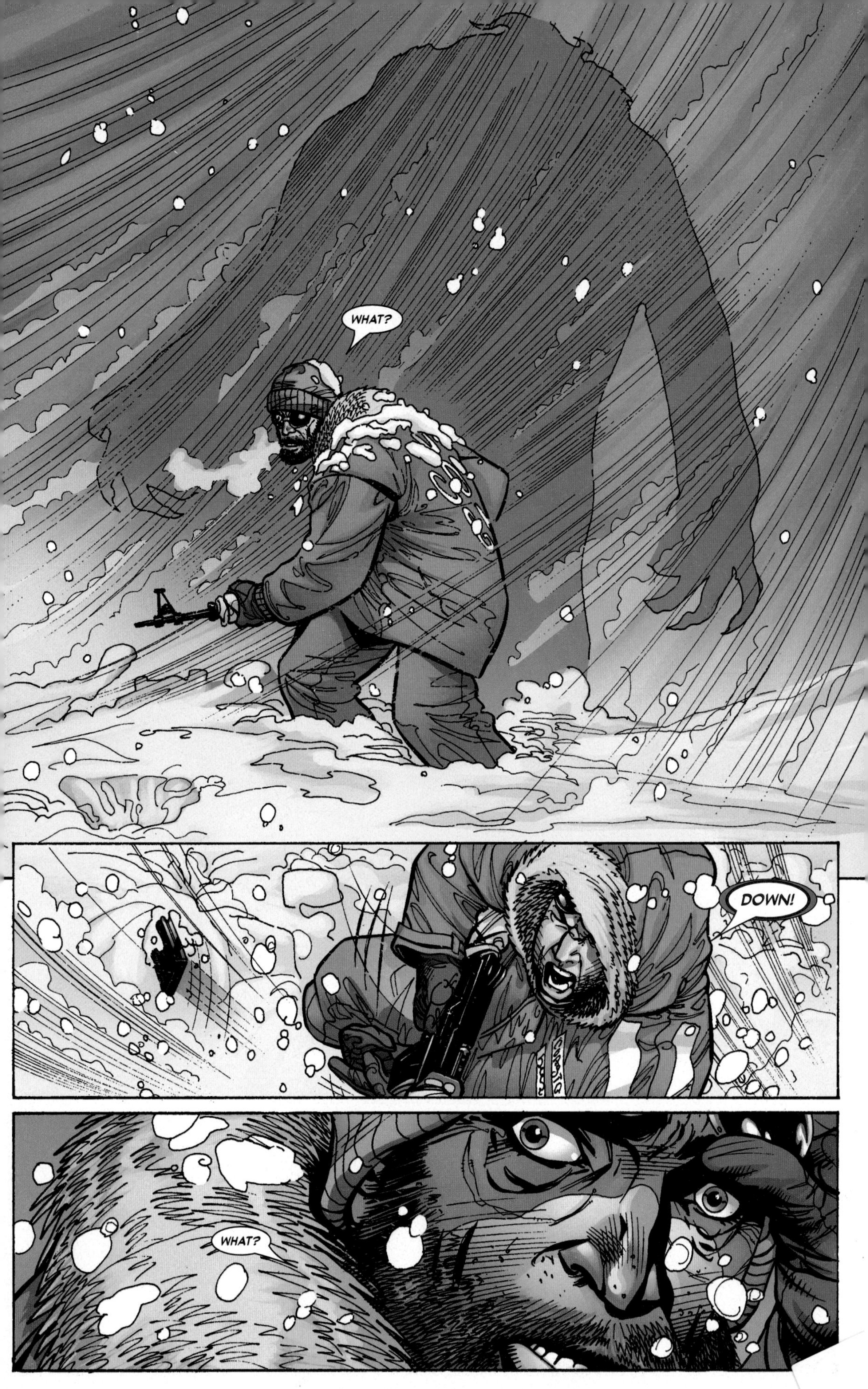
WHAT?
DOWN!
WHAT?

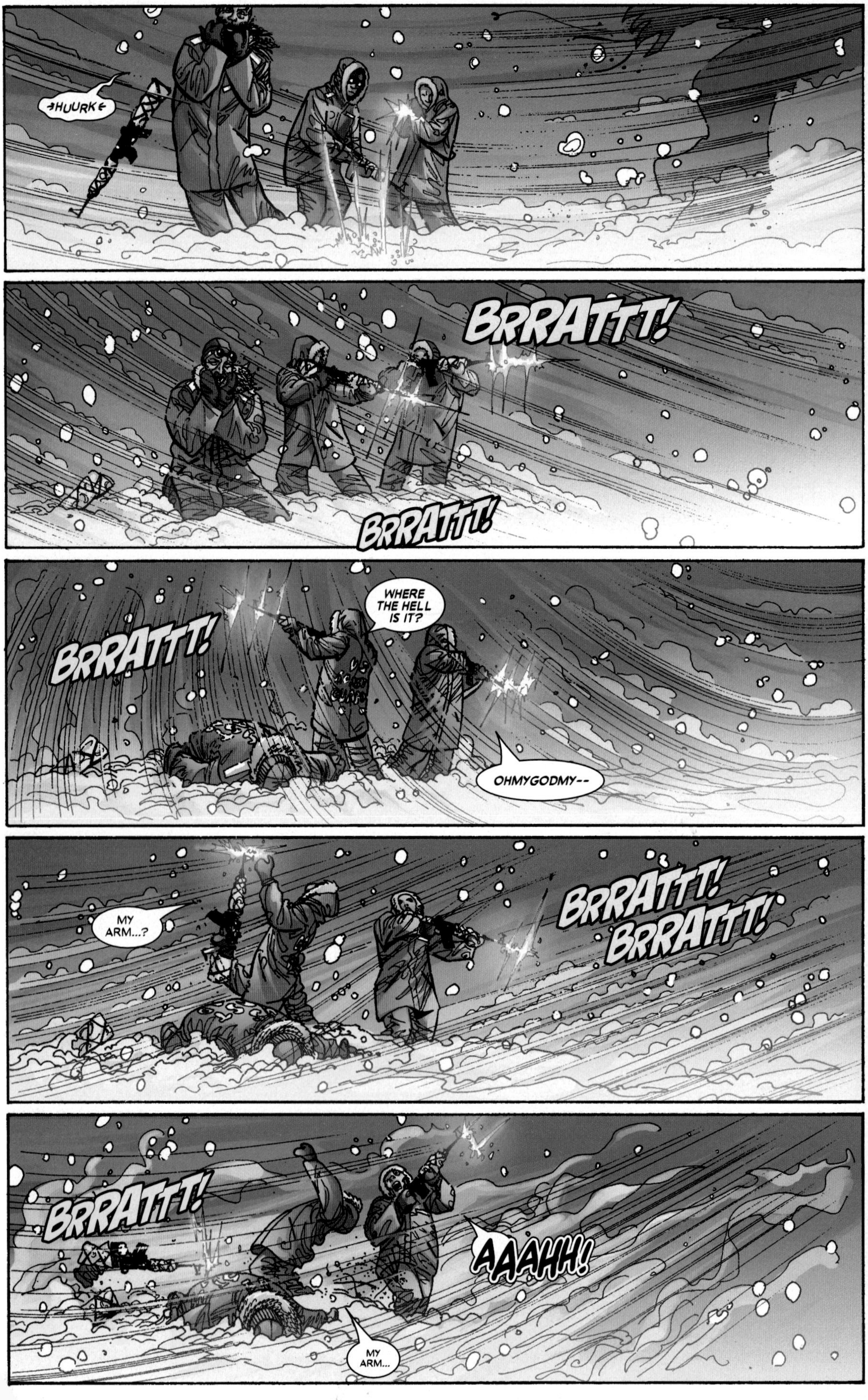
HUURK
BRRATTT!
BRRATTT!
BRRATTT!
WHERE THE HELL IS IT?
OHMYGODMY--
MY ARM...?
BRRATTT! BRRATTT!
BRRATTT!
AAAHH!
MY ARM...

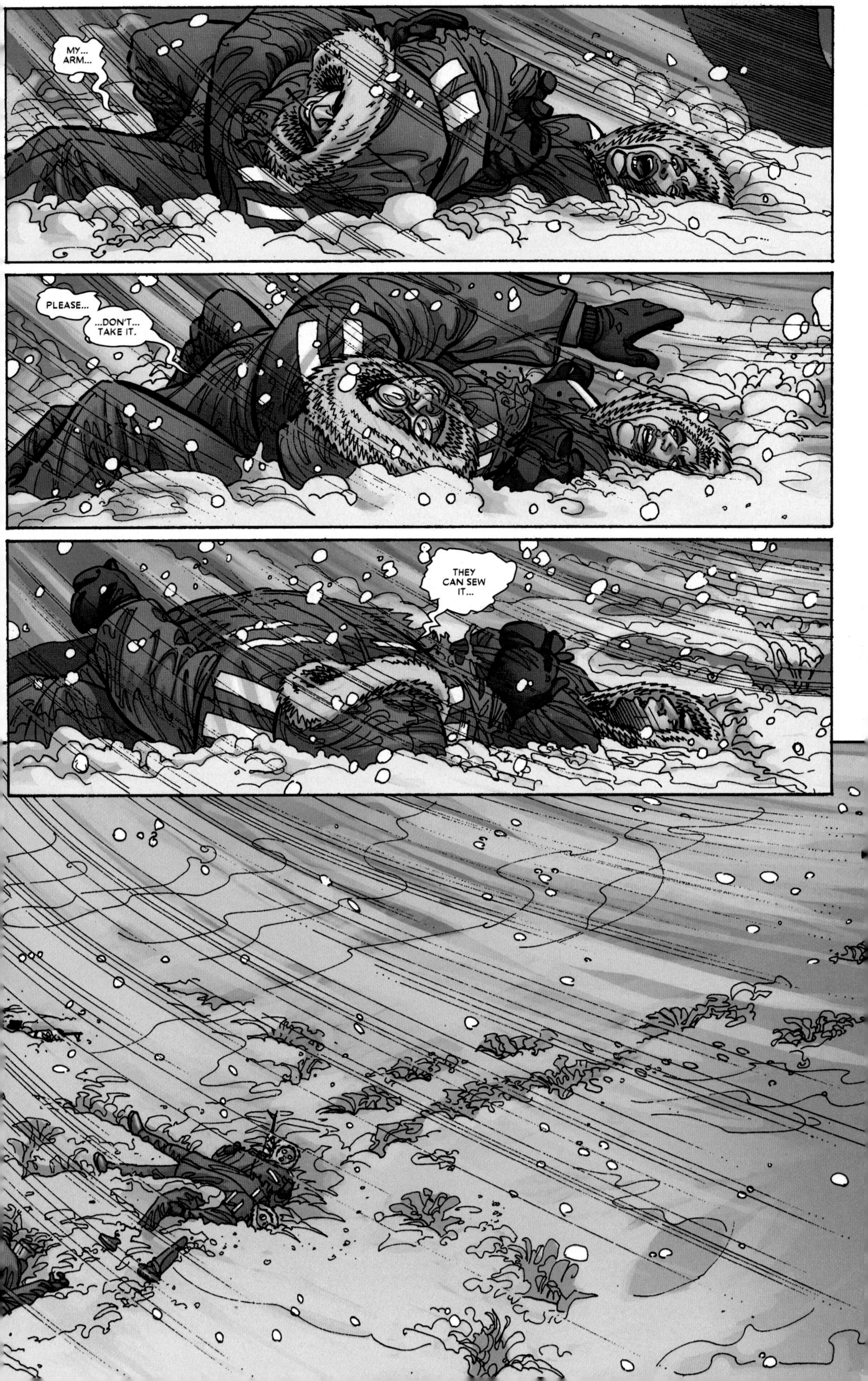
MY... ARM...
PLEASE...
...DON'T... TAKE IT.
THEY CAN SEW IT...

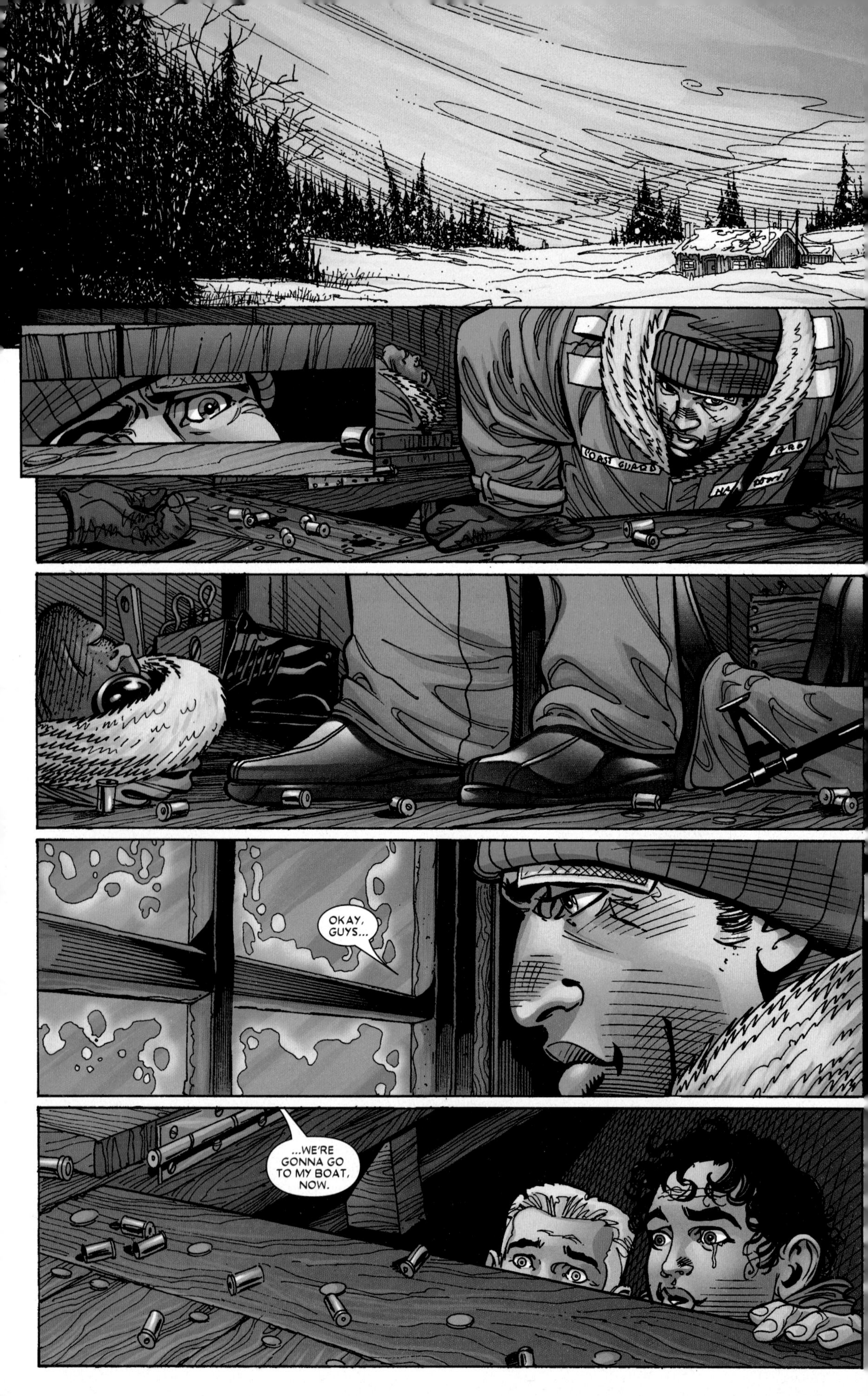
OKAY, GUYS...
...WE'RE GONNA GO TO MY BOAT, NOW.

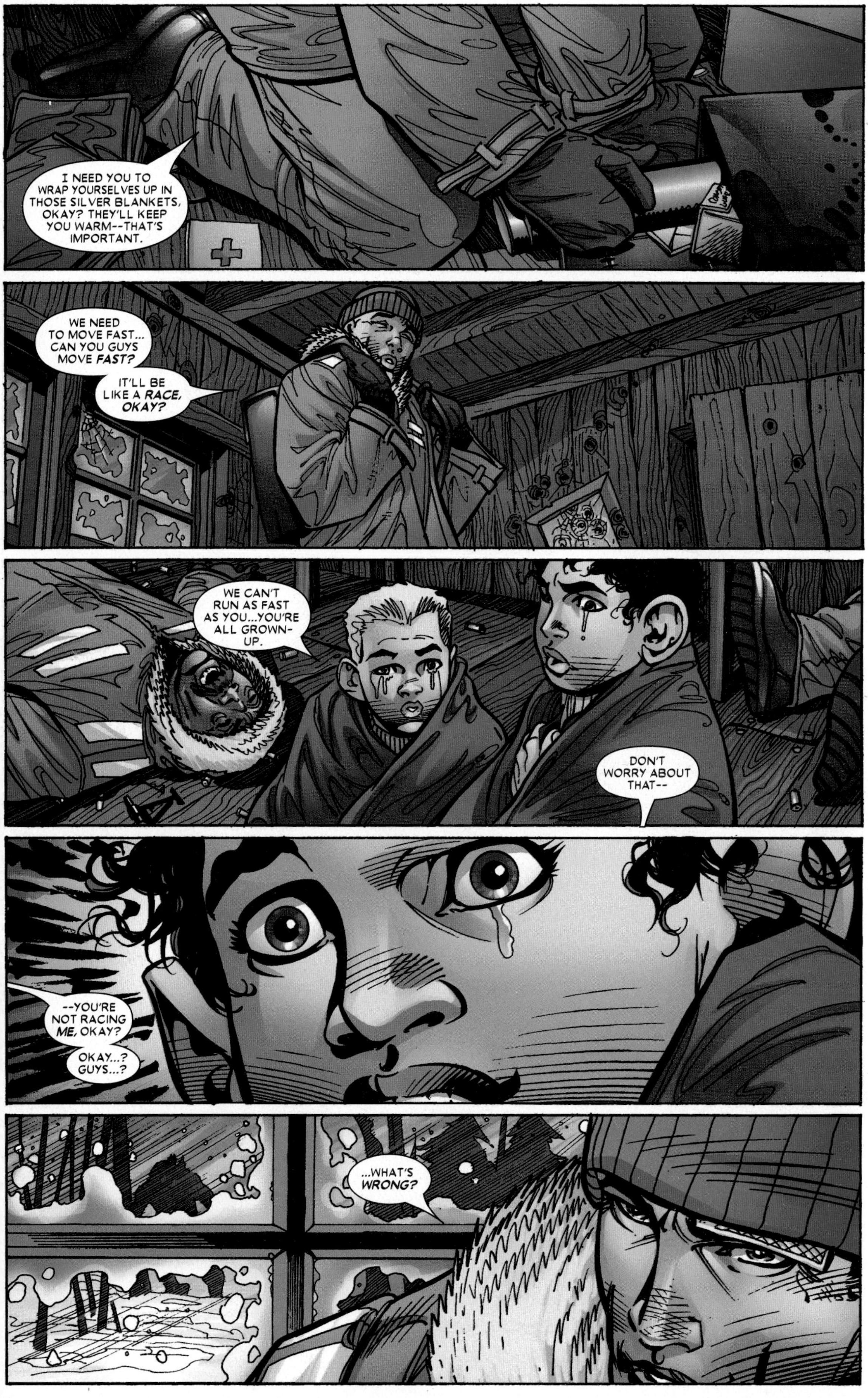
I NEED YOU TO WRAP YOURSELVES UP IN THOSE SILVER BLANKETS, OKAY? THEY'LL KEEP YOU WARM--THAT'S IMPORTANT.
WE NEED TO MOVE FAST... CAN YOU GUYS MOVE *FAST?*
IT'LL BE LIKE A *RACE, OKAY?*
WE CAN'T RUN AS FAST AS YOU...YOU'RE ALL GROWN-UP.
DON'T WORRY ABOUT THAT--
--YOU'RE NOT RACING *ME,* OKAY?
OKAY...? GUYS...?
...WHAT'S *WRONG?*

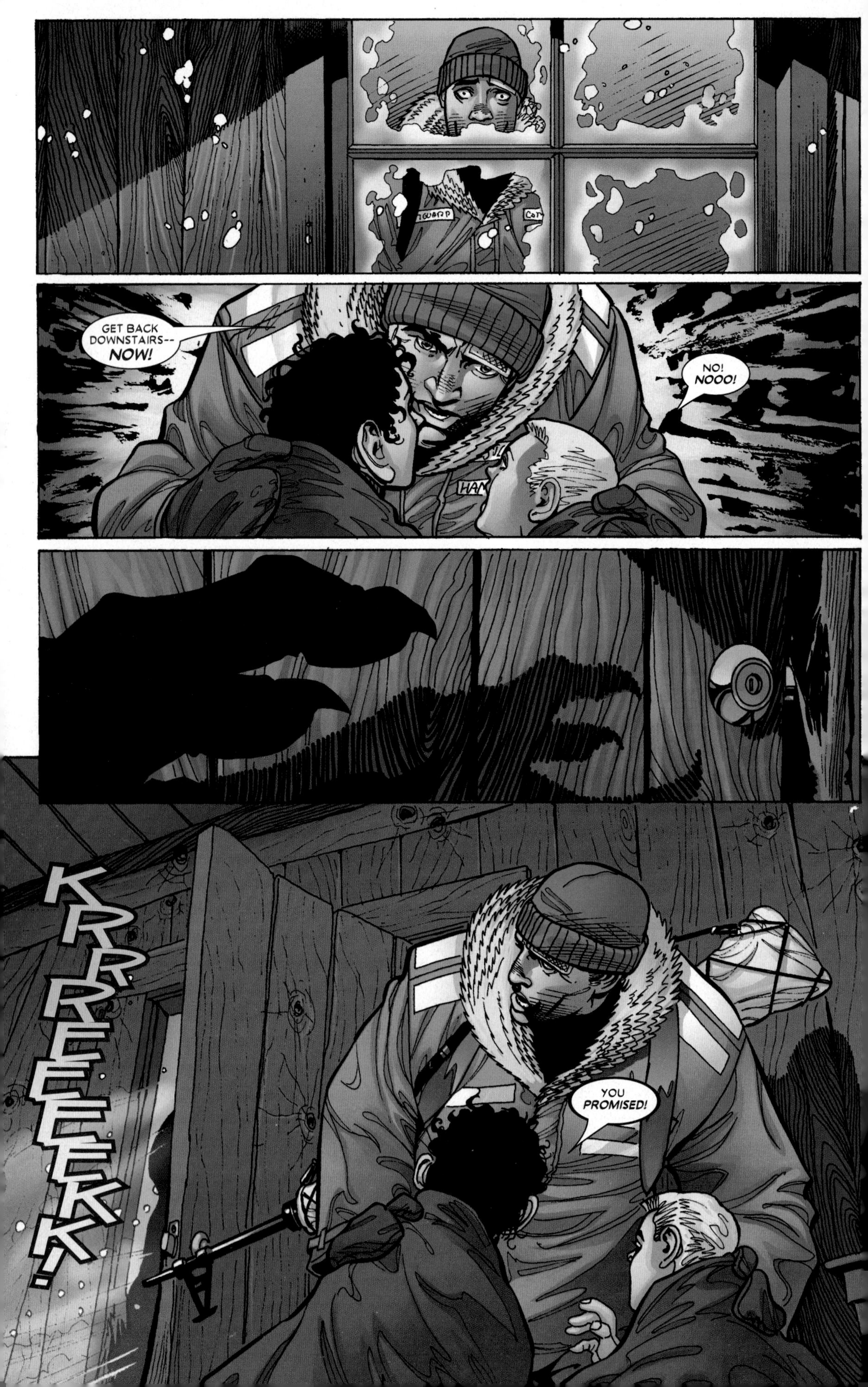
GET BACK DOWNSTAIRS-- NOW!
NO! NOOO!
KRRREEEEKK!
YOU PROMISED!

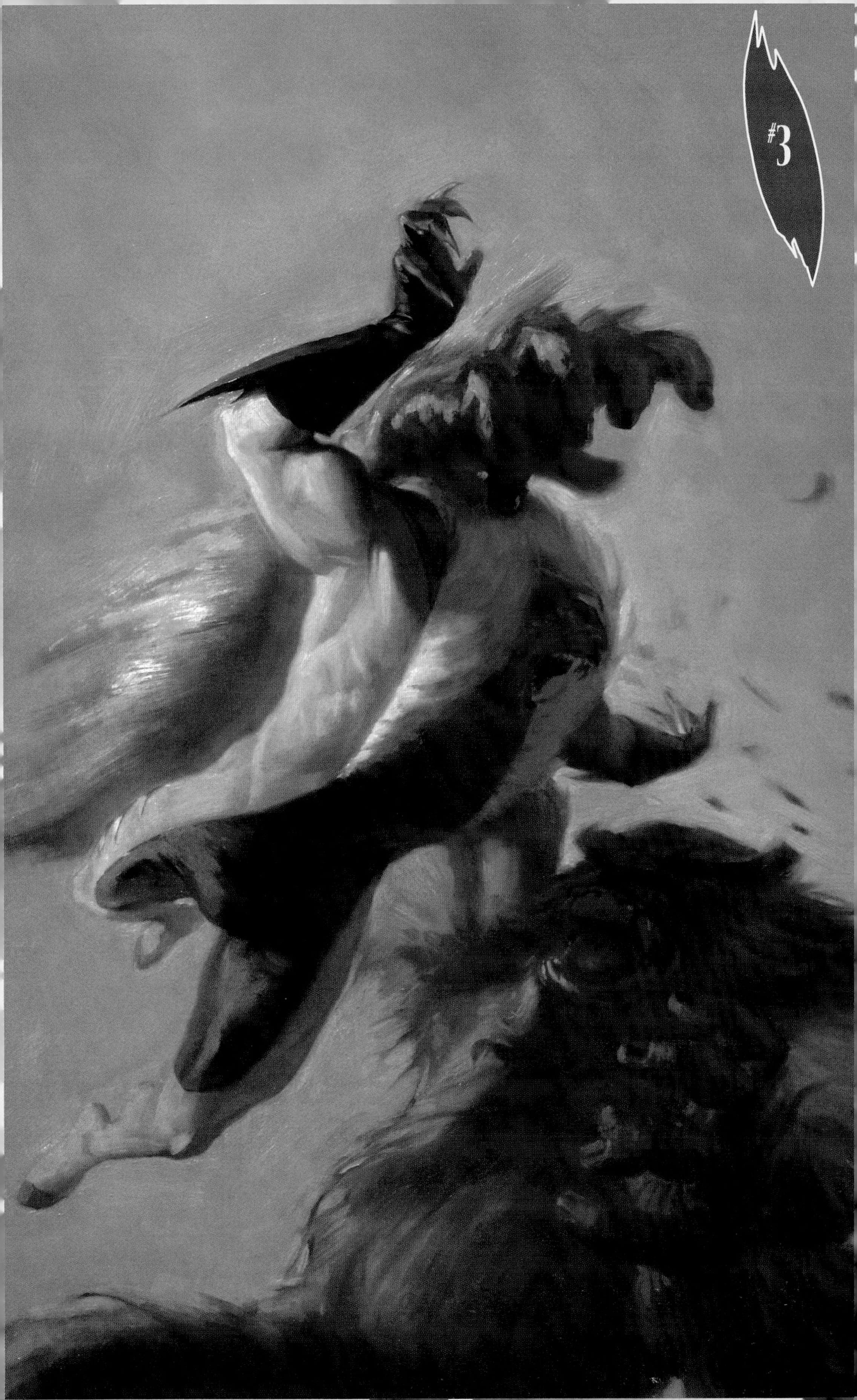
#3

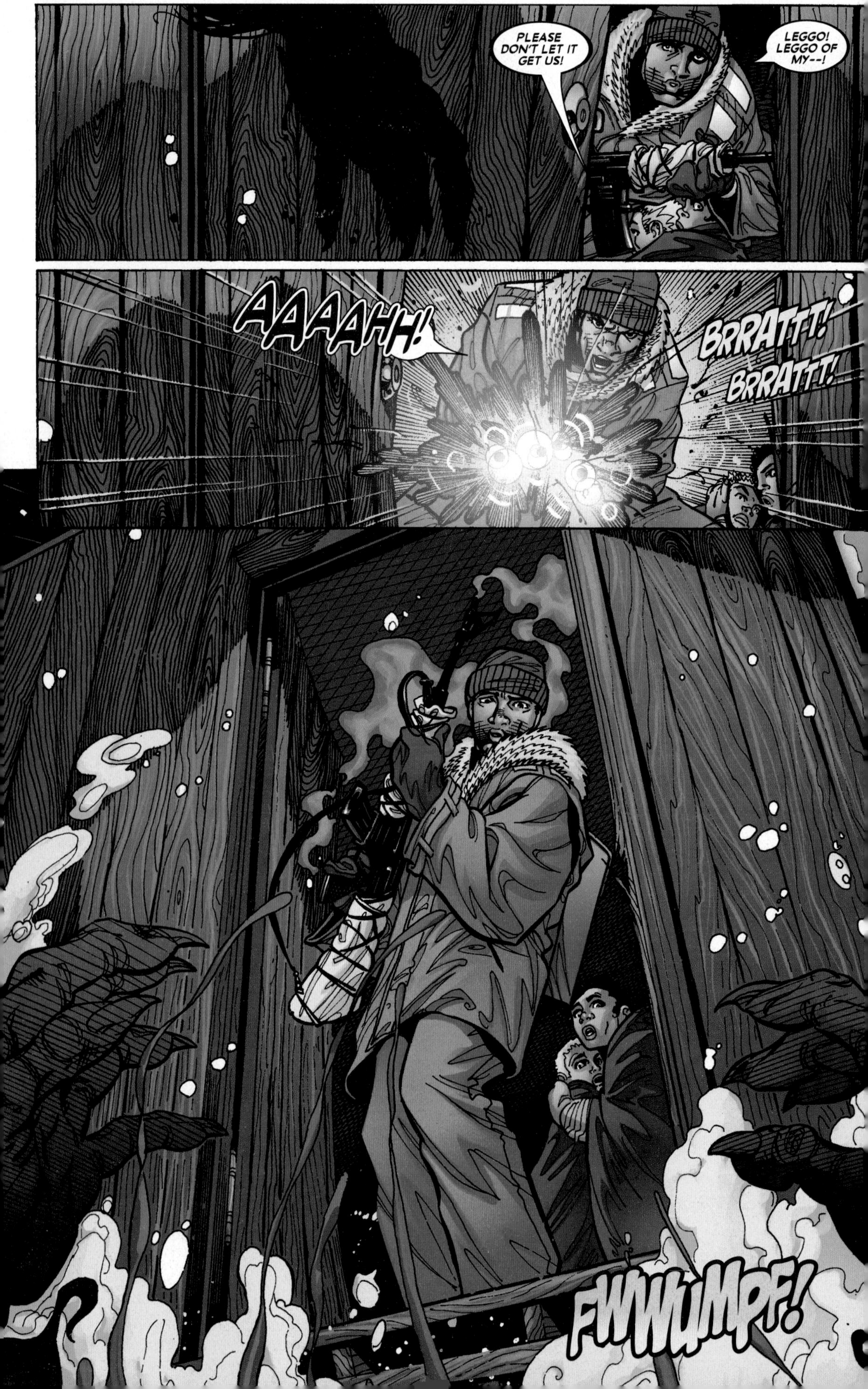
PLEASE DON'T LET IT GET US!
LEGGO! LEGGO OF MY--!
AAAAHH!
BRRATTT!
BRRATTT!
FWWUMPF!

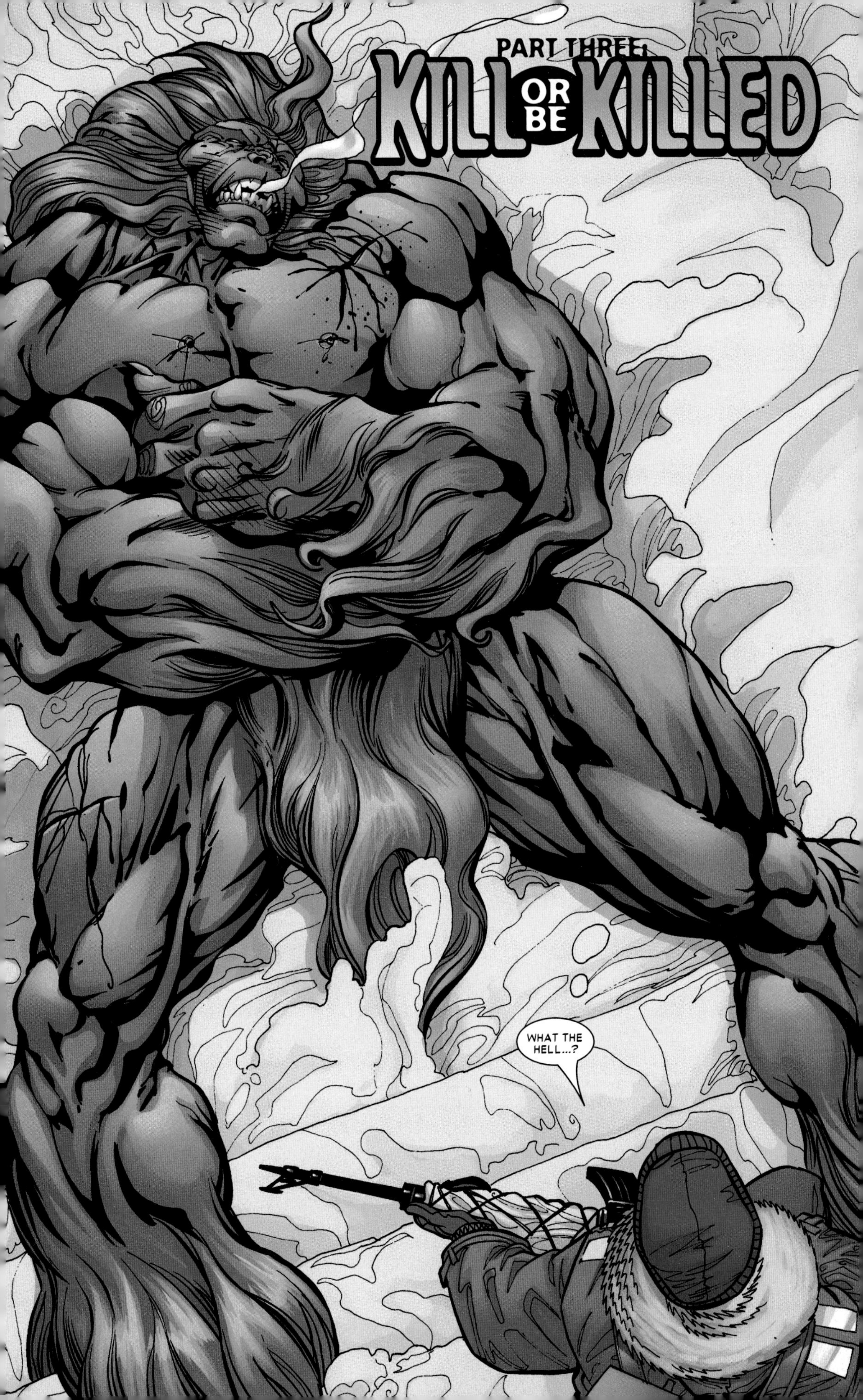
PART THREE:
KILL OR BE KILLED
WHAT THE HELL...?

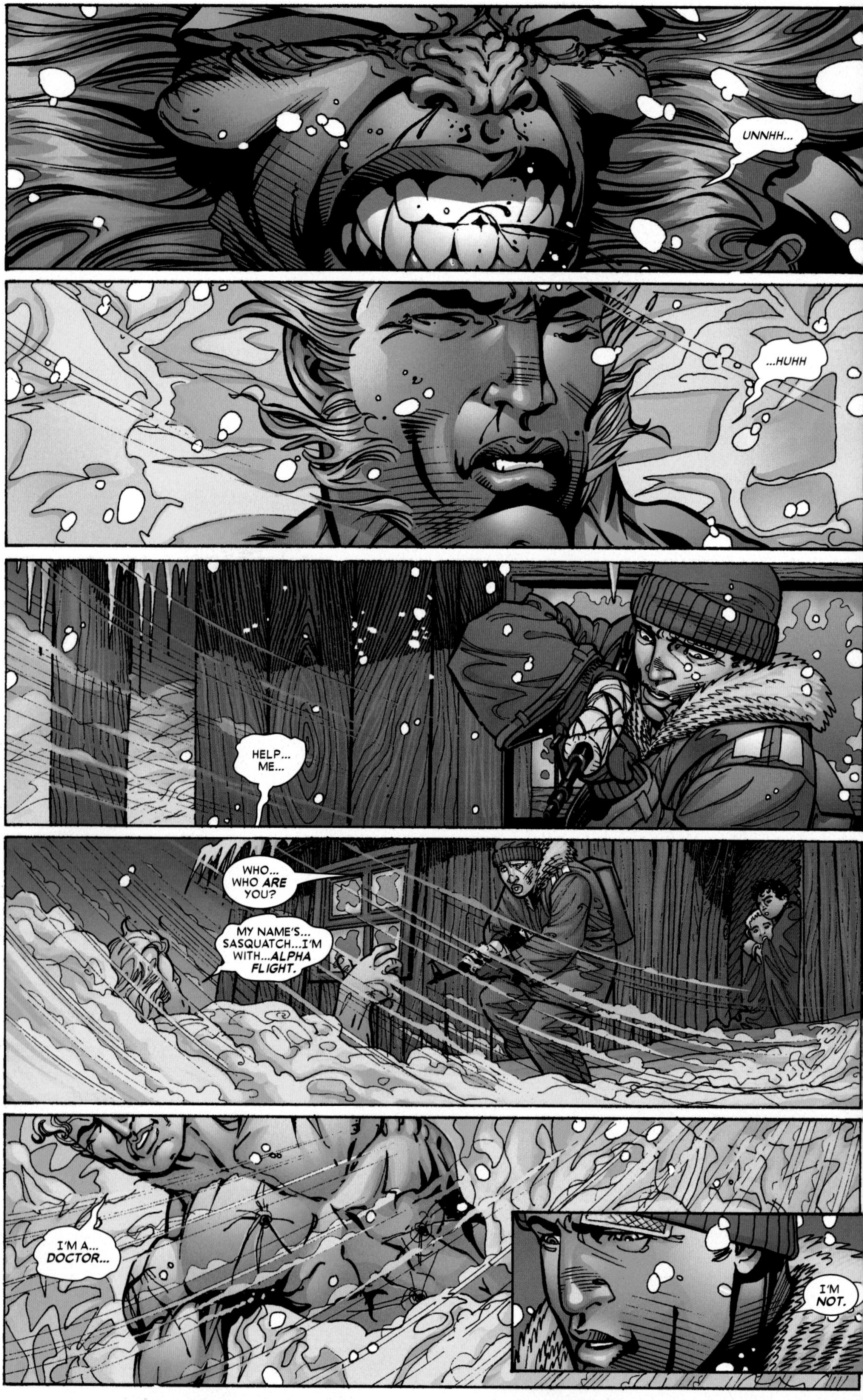
UNNHH...
...HUHH
HELP... ME...
WHO... WHO ARE YOU?
MY NAME'S... SASQUATCH...I'M WITH...ALPHA FLIGHT.
I'M A... DOCTOR...
I'M NOT.

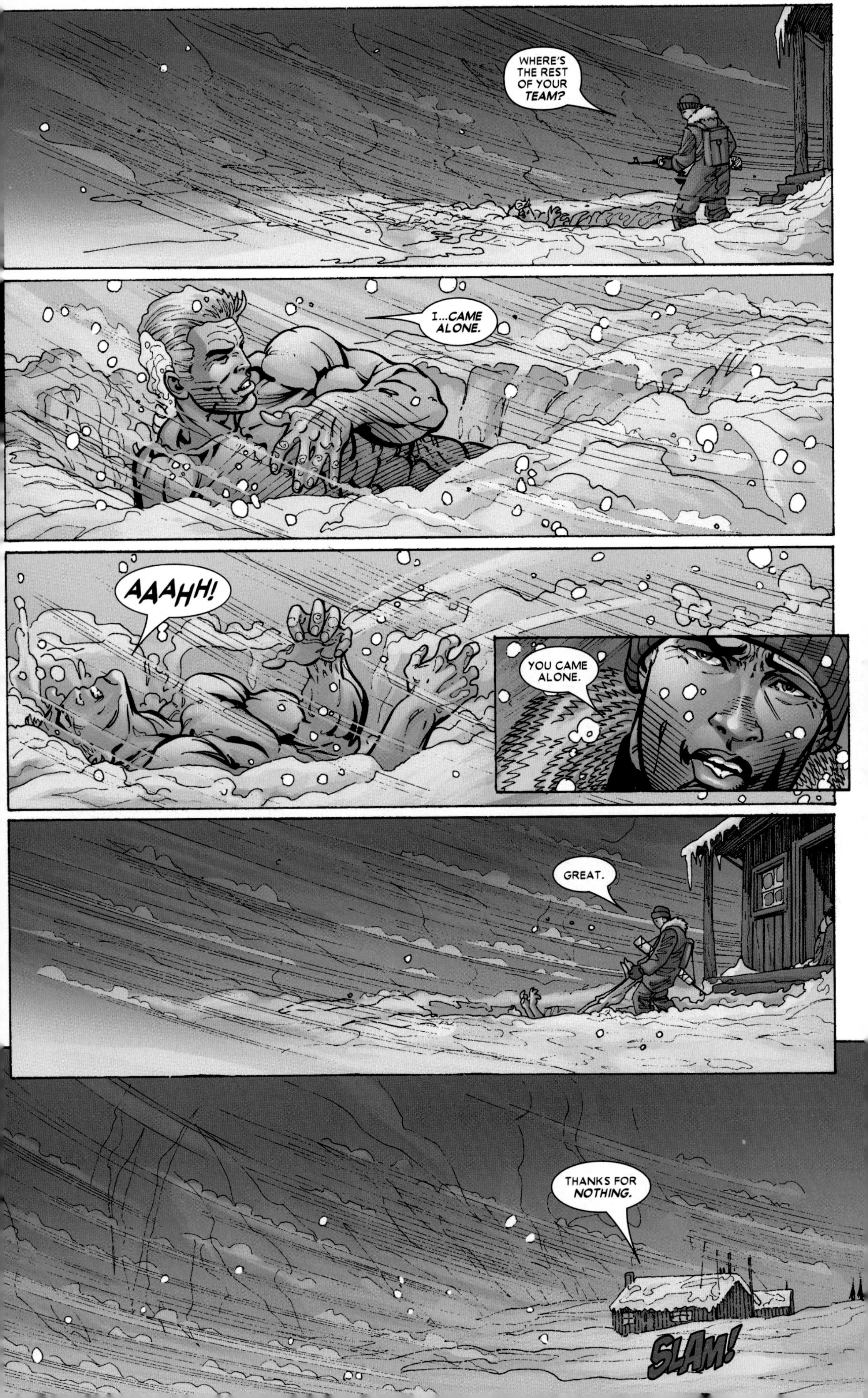
WHERE'S THE REST OF YOUR *TEAM?*
I...*CAME ALONE.*
AAAHH!
YOU CAME ALONE.
GREAT.
THANKS FOR *NOTHING.*
SLAM!

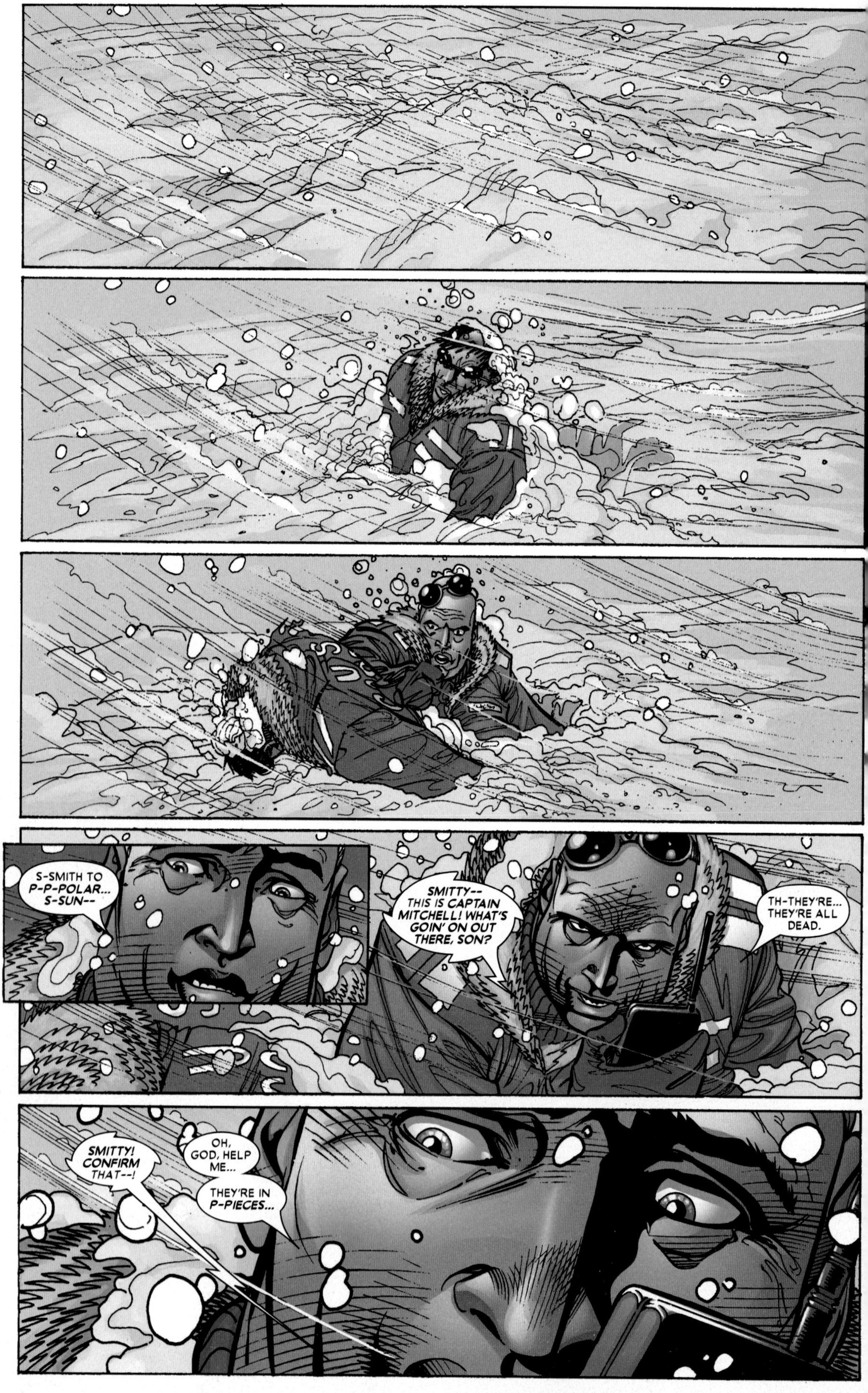
S-SMITH TO P-P-POLAR... S-SUN--
SMITTY-- THIS IS CAPTAIN MITCHELL! WHAT'S GOIN' ON OUT THERE, SON?
TH-THEY'RE... THEY'RE ALL DEAD.
SMITTY! CONFIRM THAT--!
OH, GOD, HELP ME...
THEY'RE IN P-PIECES...

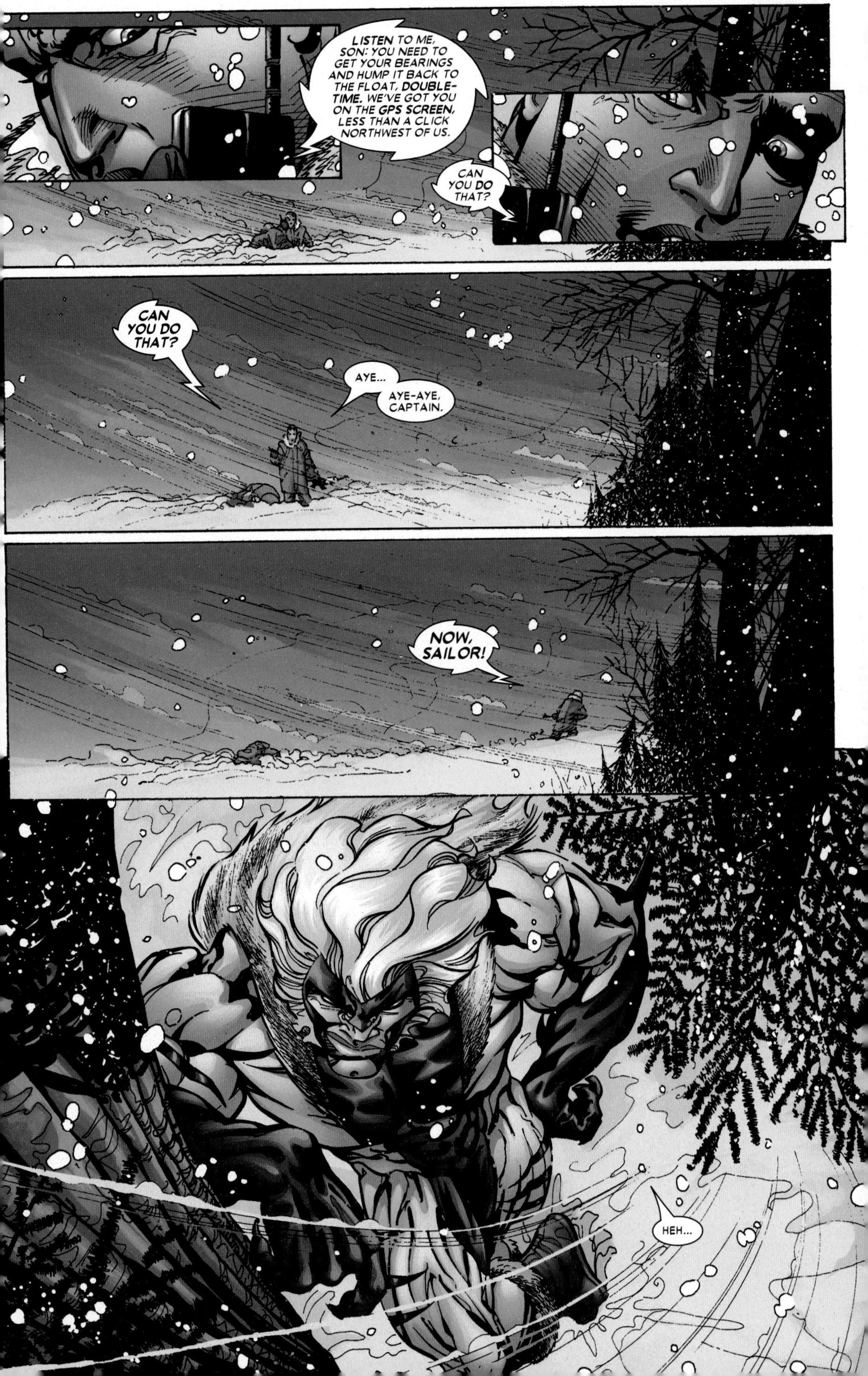
LISTEN TO ME, SON: YOU NEED TO GET YOUR BEARINGS AND HUMP IT BACK TO THE FLOAT, DOUBLE-TIME. WE'VE GOT YOU ON THE GPS SCREEN, LESS THAN A CLICK NORTHWEST OF US.
CAN YOU DO THAT?
CAN YOU DO THAT?
AYE...
AYE-AYE, CAPTAIN.
NOW, SAILOR!
HEH...

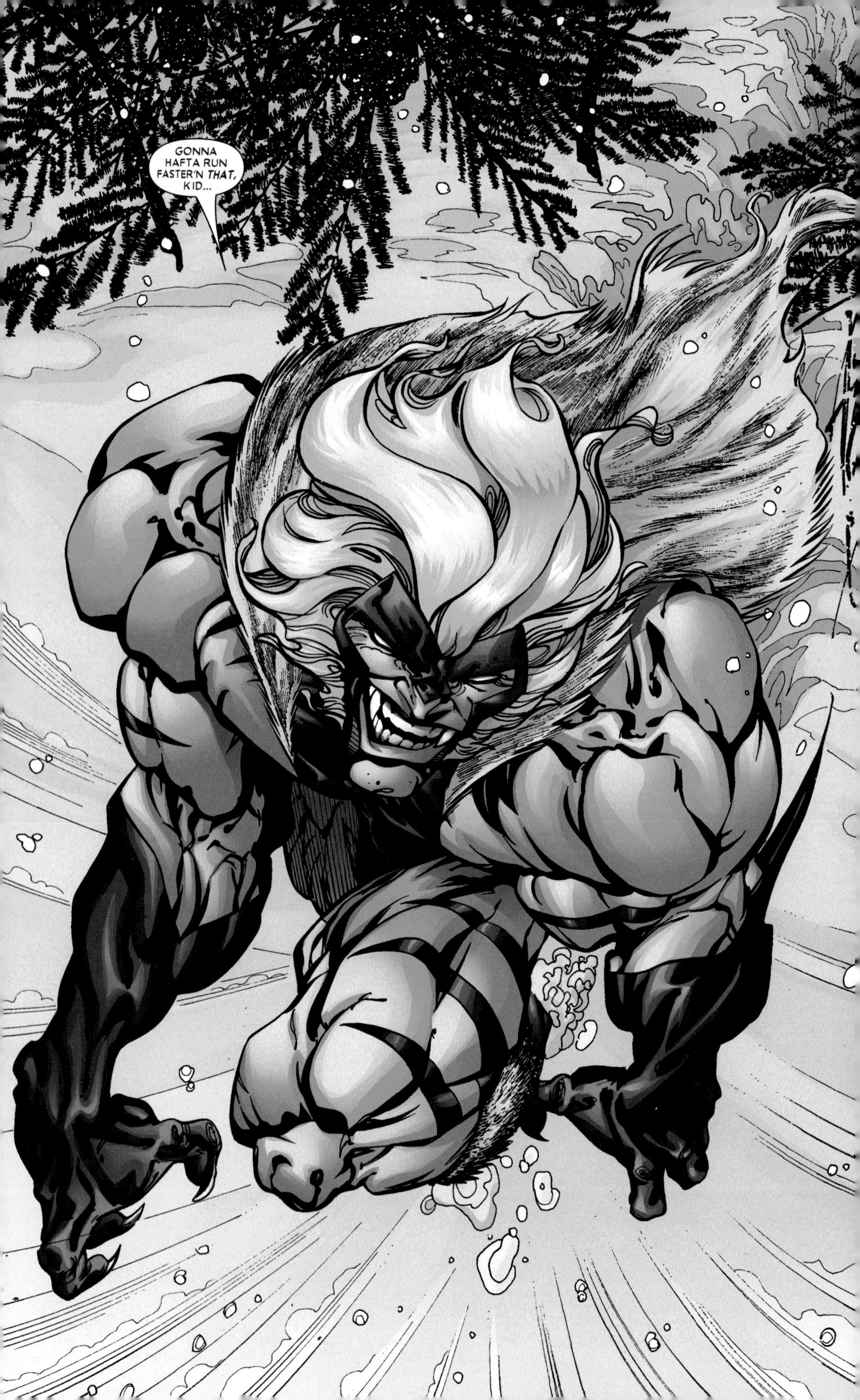
GONNA HAFTA RUN FASTER'N THAT, KID...

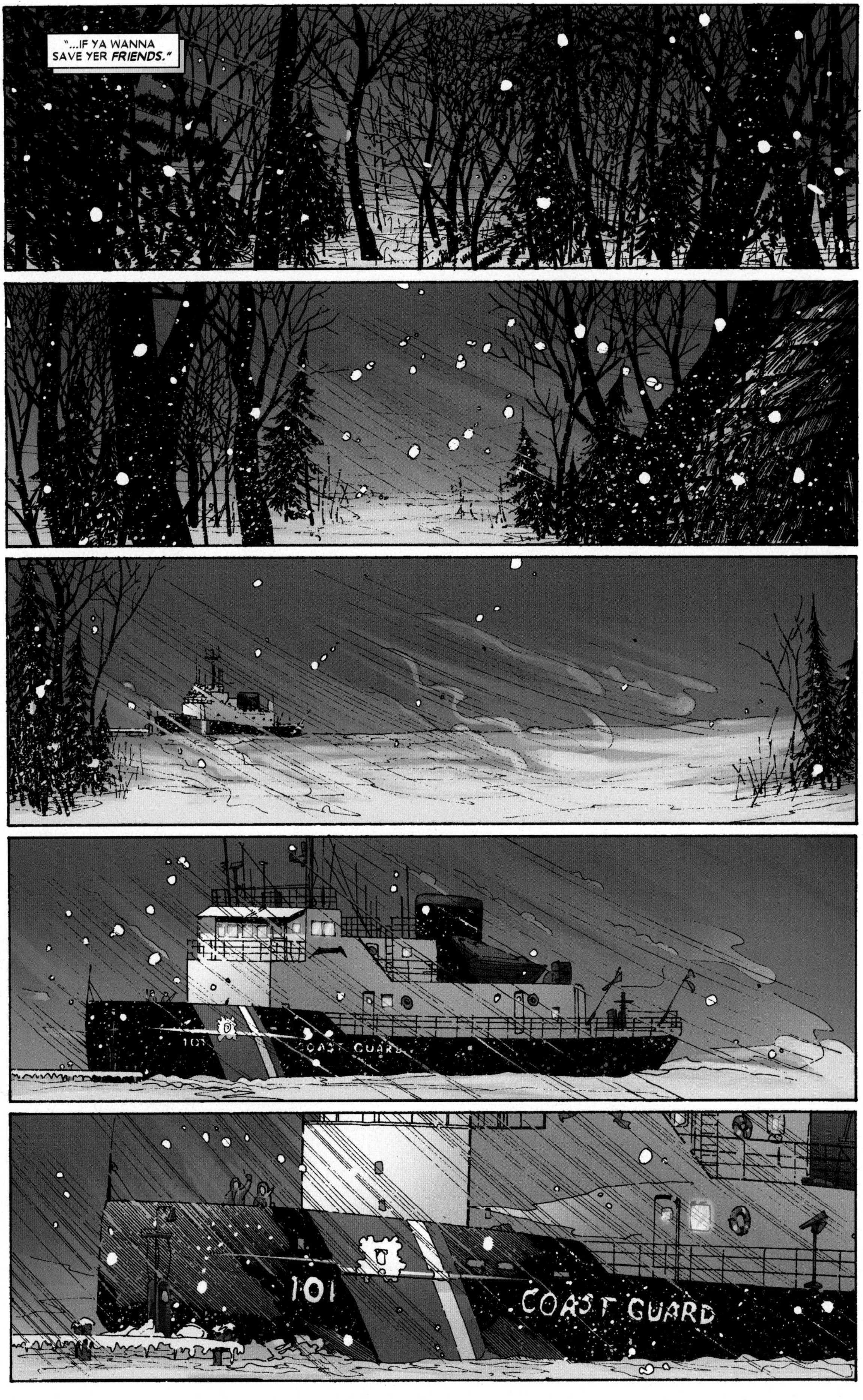
"...IF YA WANNA SAVE YER FRIENDS."
101
COAST GUARD
101
COAST GUARD

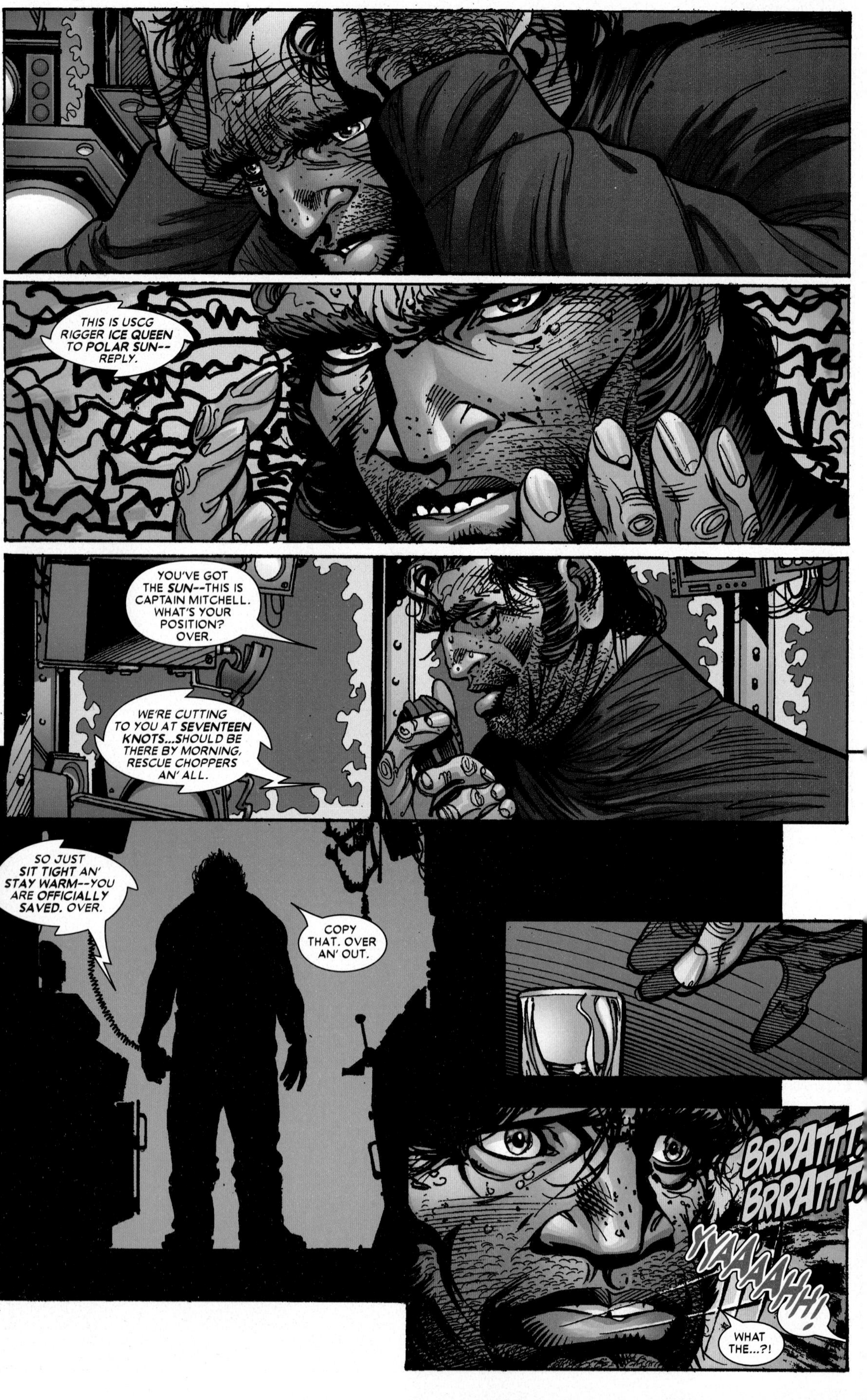
THIS IS USCG RIGGER ICE QUEEN TO POLAR SUN-- REPLY.
YOU'VE GOT THE SUN--THIS IS CAPTAIN MITCHELL. WHAT'S YOUR POSITION? OVER.
WE'RE CUTTING TO YOU AT SEVENTEEN KNOTS...SHOULD BE THERE BY MORNING, RESCUE CHOPPERS AN' ALL.
SO JUST SIT TIGHT AN' STAY WARM--YOU ARE OFFICIALLY SAVED. OVER.
COPY THAT. OVER AN' OUT.
BRRATT! BRRATT!
YYAAAAHH!
WHAT THE...?!

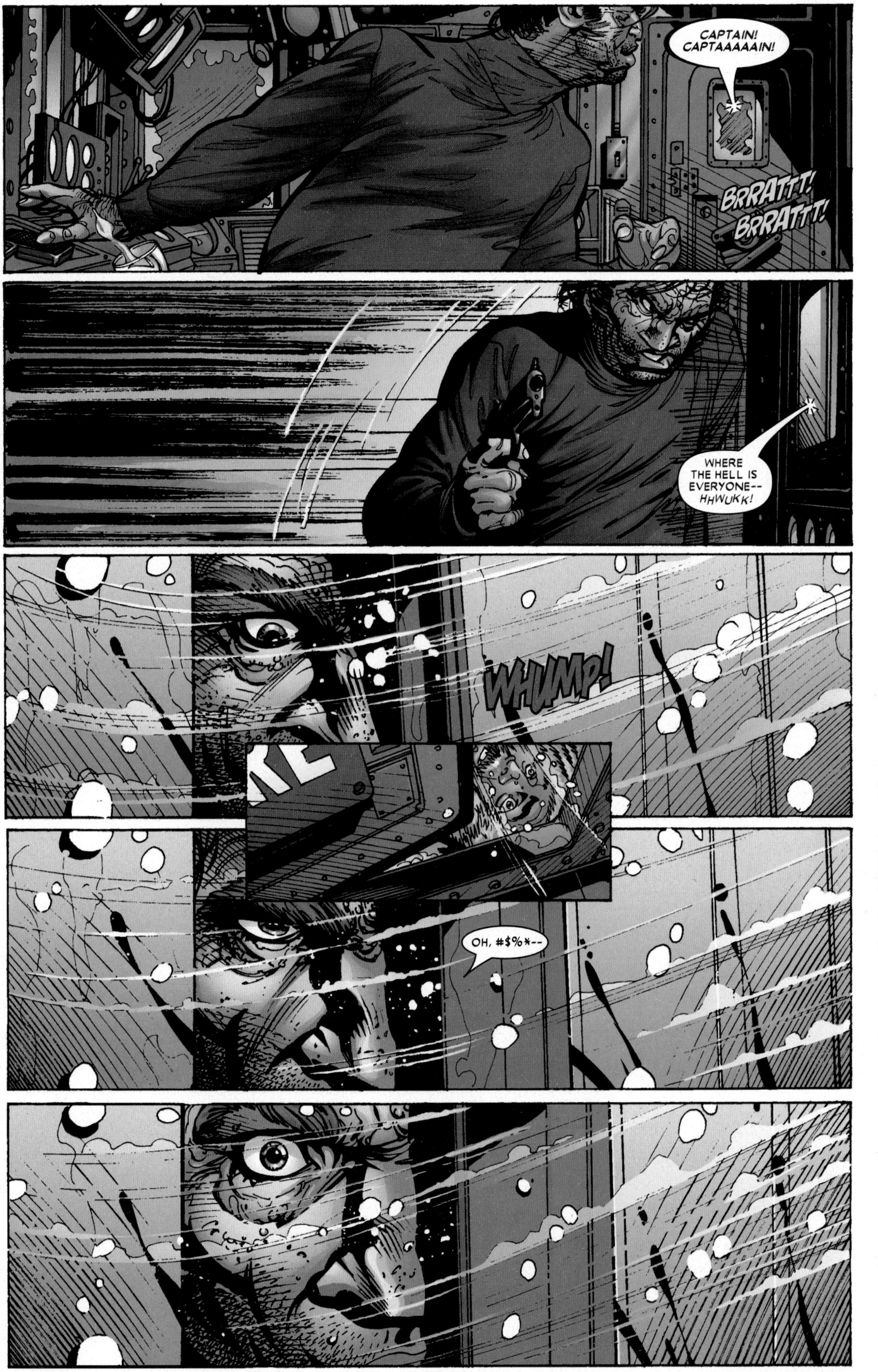
CAPTAIN! CAPTAAAAAIN!
BRRATTT! BRRATTT!
WHERE THE HELL IS EVERYONE-- HHWUKK!
WHUMP!
OH, #$%*--

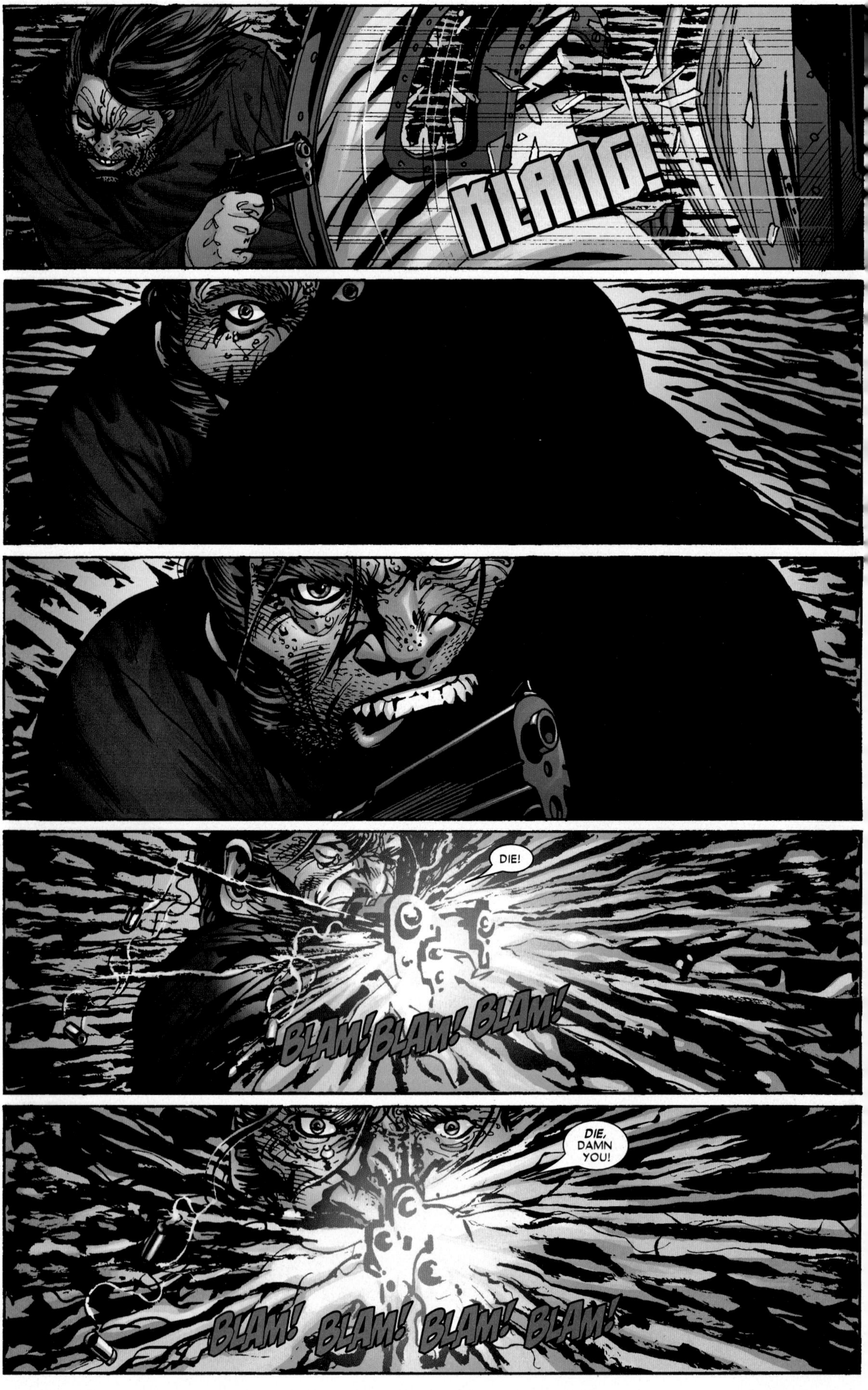
KLANG!
DIE!
BLAM! BLAM! BLAM!
DIE, DAMN YOU!
BLAM! BLAM! BLAM! BLAM!

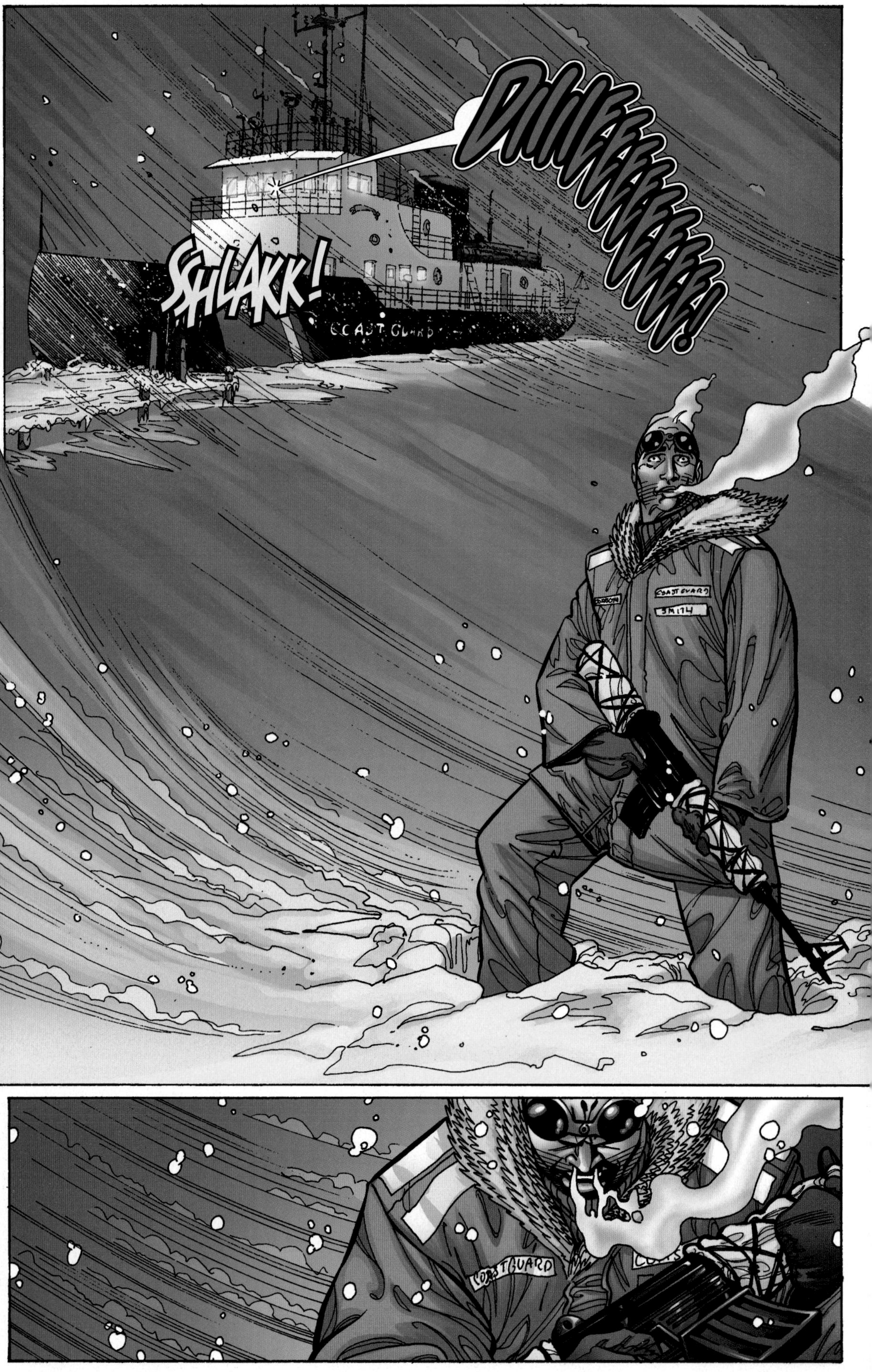
SHLAKK!
COAST GUARD
COAST GUARD
SMITH
COAST GUARD

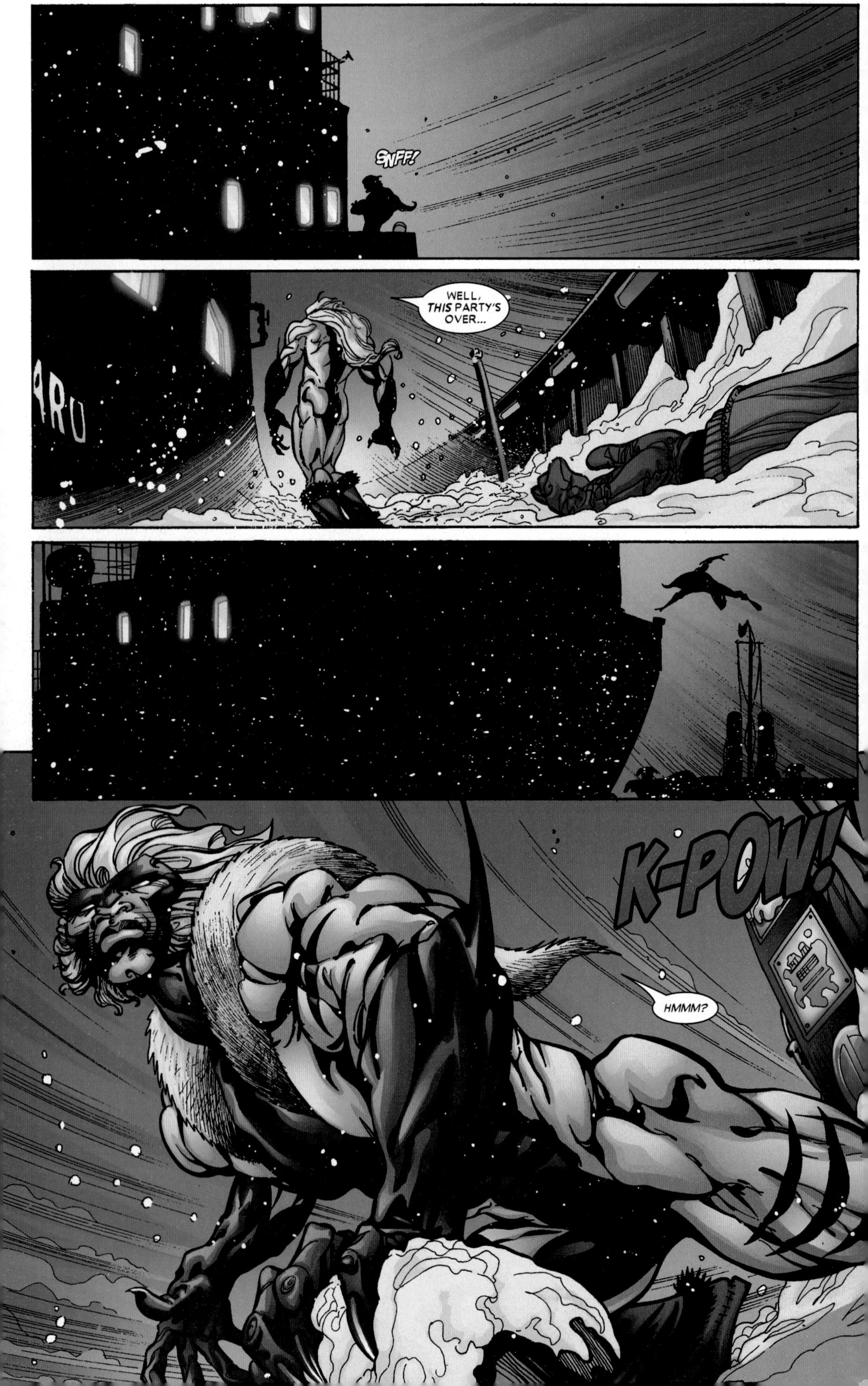
SNFF!
WELL, THIS PARTY'S OVER...
K-POW!
HMMM?

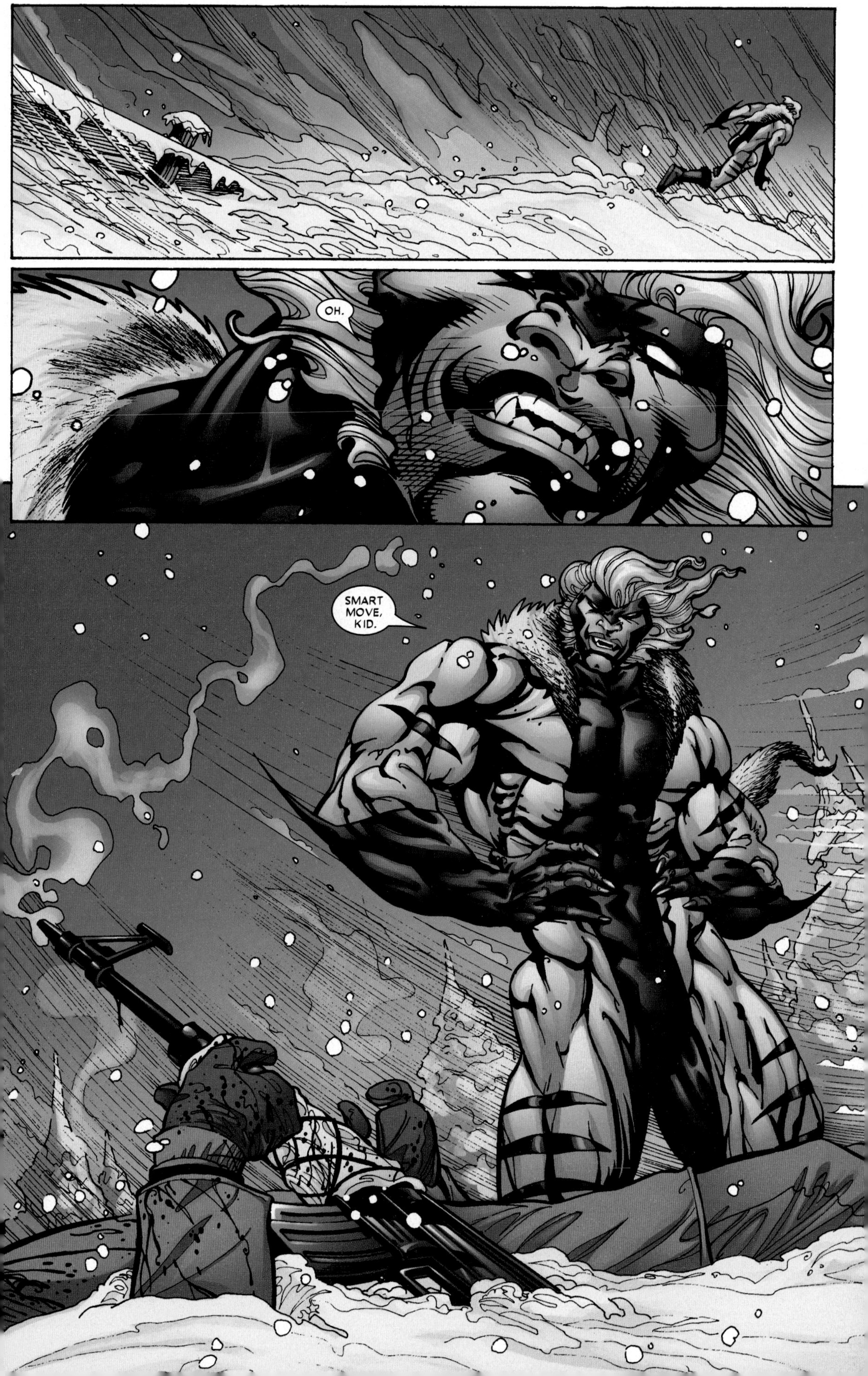
OH.
SMART MOVE, KID.

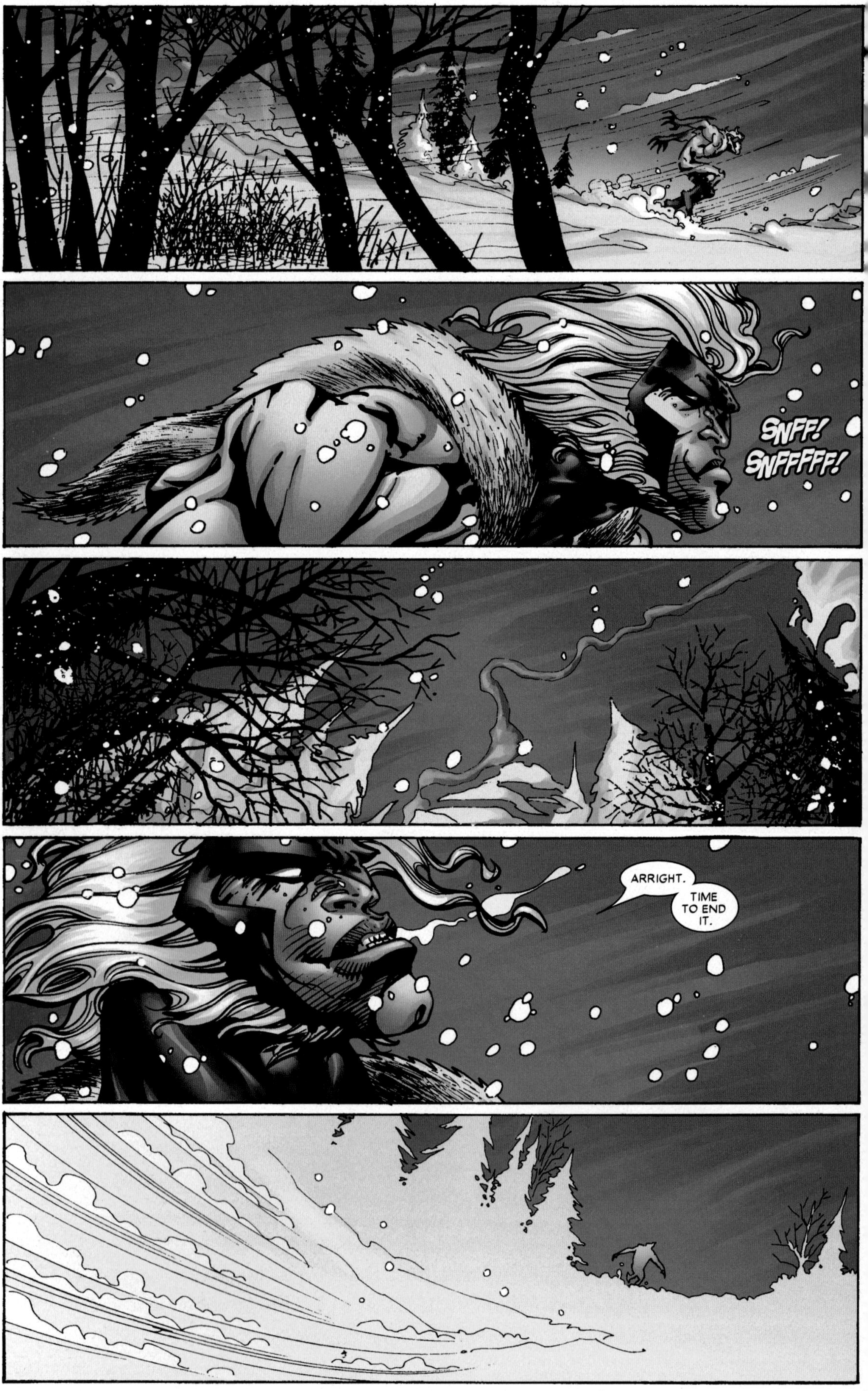
SNFF!
SNFFFFF!
ARRIGHT.
TIME TO END IT.

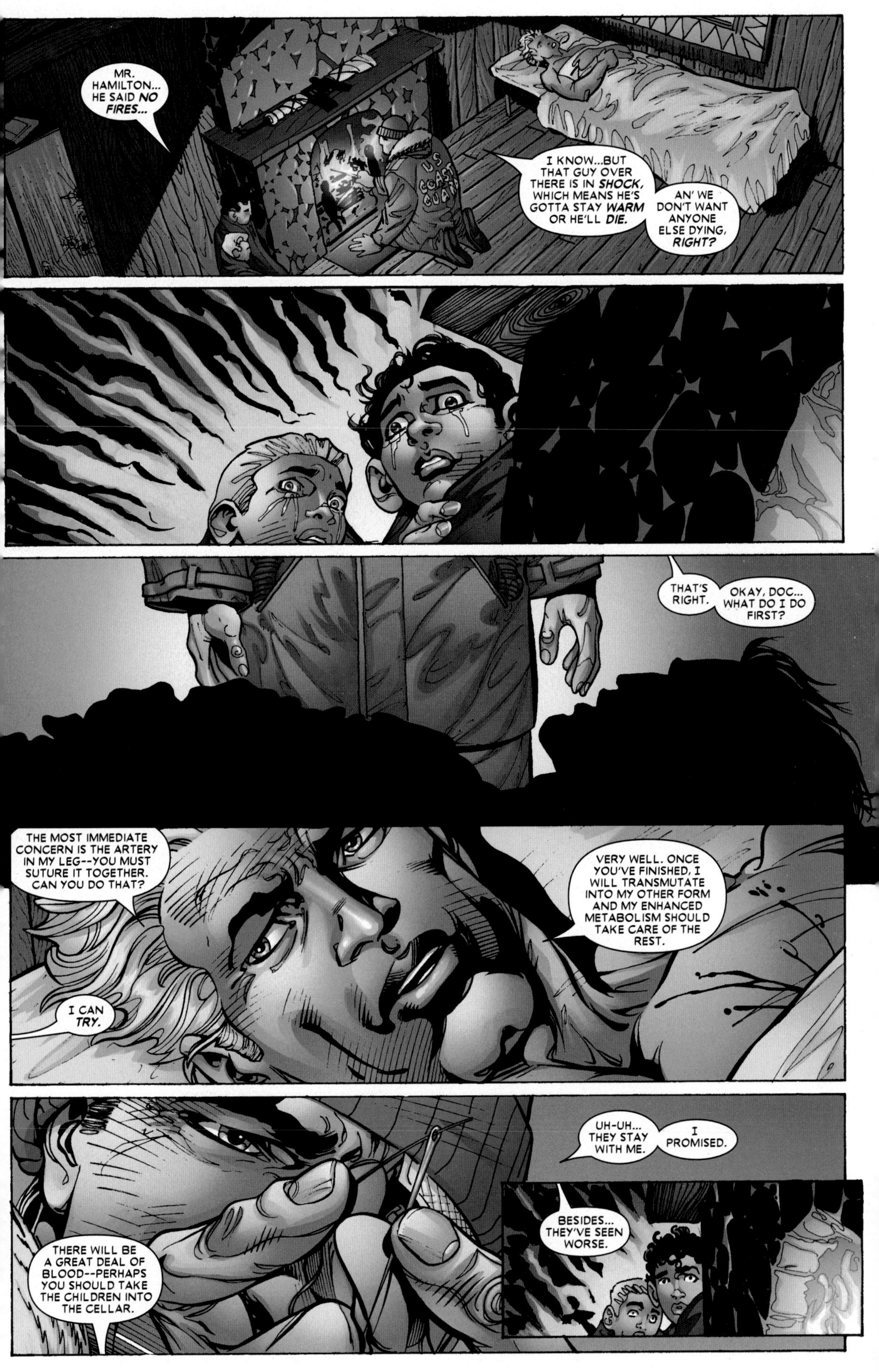
MR. HAMILTON... HE SAID NO FIRES...
I KNOW...BUT THAT GUY OVER THERE IS IN SHOCK, WHICH MEANS HE'S GOTTA STAY WARM OR HE'LL DIE.
AN' WE DON'T WANT ANYONE ELSE DYING, RIGHT?
U S COAST GUARD
THAT'S RIGHT.
OKAY, DOC... WHAT DO I DO FIRST?
THE MOST IMMEDIATE CONCERN IS THE ARTERY IN MY LEG--YOU MUST SUTURE IT TOGETHER. CAN YOU DO THAT?
I CAN TRY.
VERY WELL. ONCE YOU'VE FINISHED, I WILL TRANSMUTATE INTO MY OTHER FORM AND MY ENHANCED METABOLISM SHOULD TAKE CARE OF THE REST.
THERE WILL BE A GREAT DEAL OF BLOOD--PERHAPS YOU SHOULD TAKE THE CHILDREN INTO THE CELLAR.
UH-UH... THEY STAY WITH ME.
I PROMISED.
BESIDES... THEY'VE SEEN WORSE.

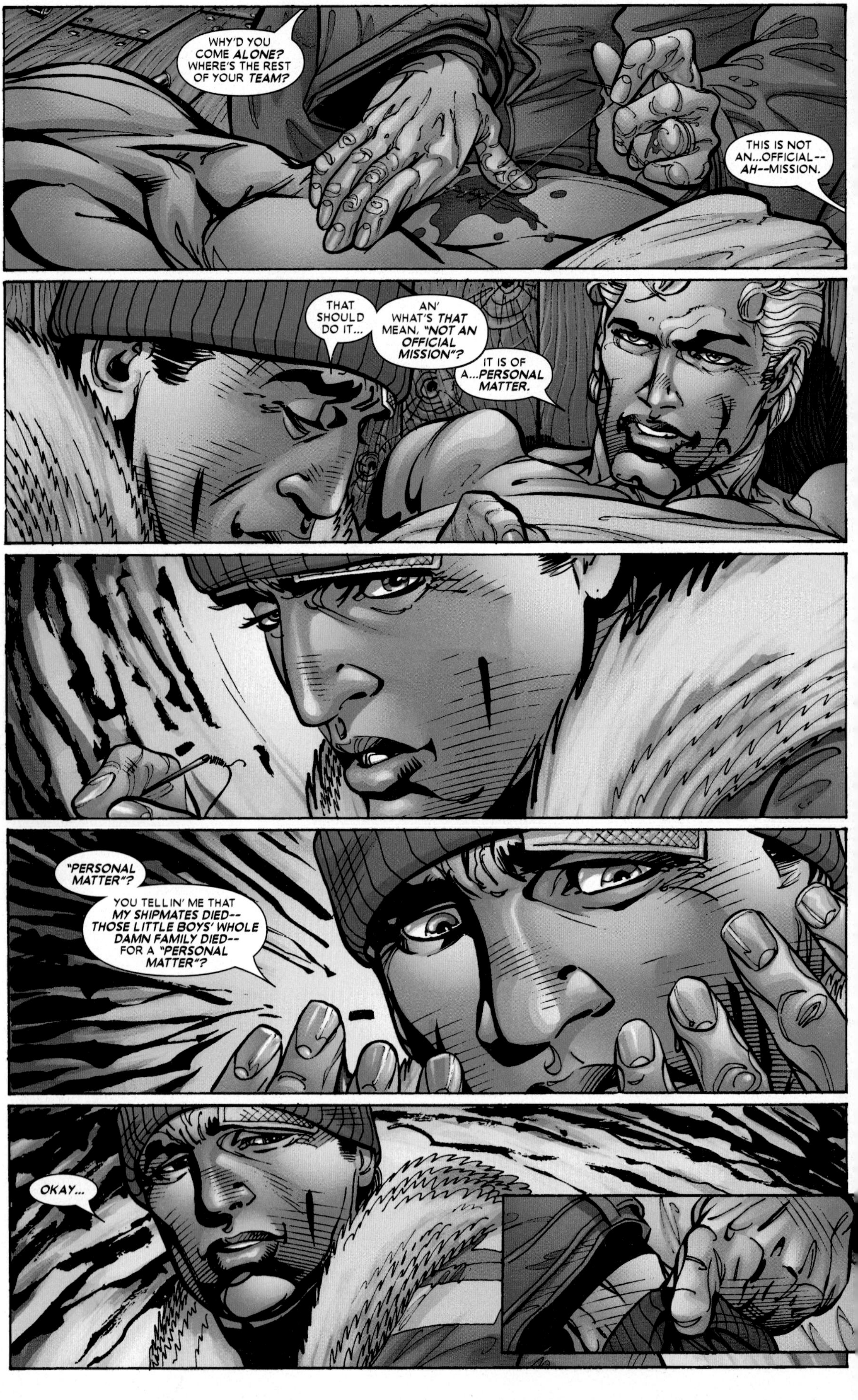

WHY'D YOU COME ALONE? WHERE'S THE REST OF YOUR TEAM?
THIS IS NOT AN...OFFICIAL--AH--MISSION.
THAT SHOULD DO IT...
AN' WHAT'S THAT MEAN, "NOT AN OFFICIAL MISSION"?
IT IS OF A...PERSONAL MATTER.
"PERSONAL MATTER"?
YOU TELLIN' ME THAT MY SHIPMATES DIED-- THOSE LITTLE BOYS' WHOLE DAMN FAMILY DIED-- FOR A "PERSONAL MATTER"?
OKAY...

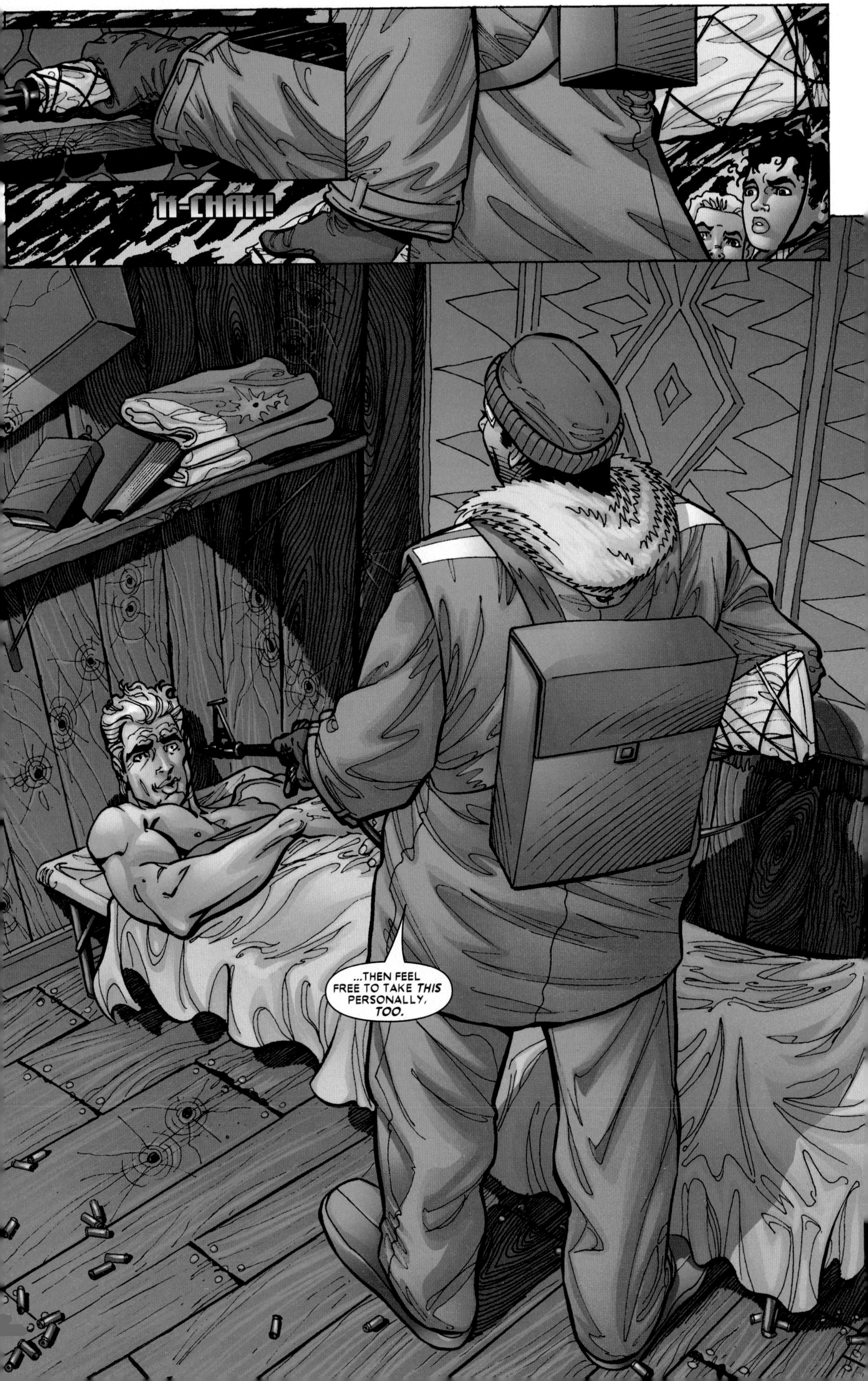
K-CHAK!
...THEN FEEL FREE TO TAKE *THIS* PERSONALLY, *TOO.*

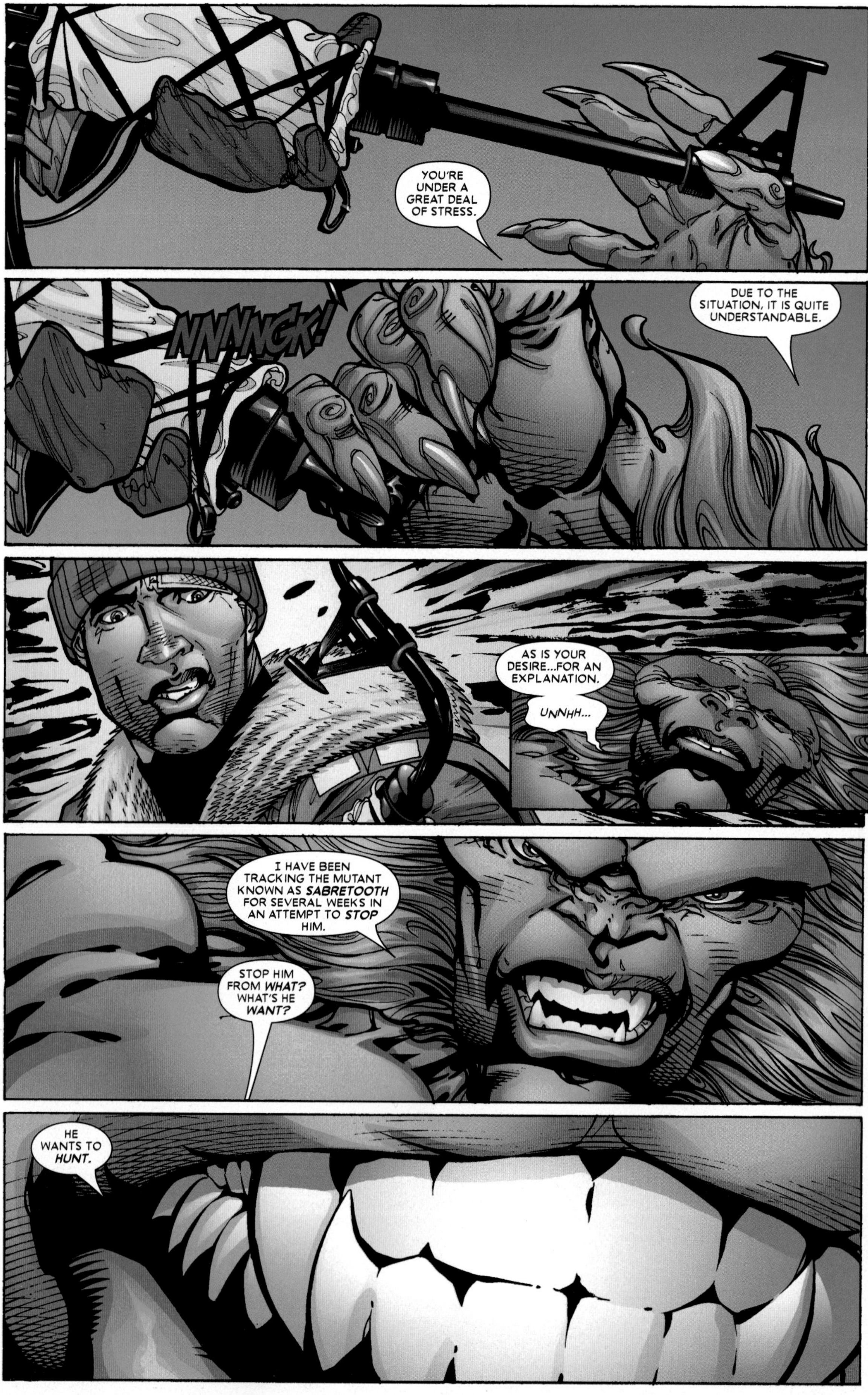
YOU'RE UNDER A GREAT DEAL OF STRESS.
NNNNGK!
DUE TO THE SITUATION, IT IS QUITE UNDERSTANDABLE.
AS IS YOUR DESIRE...FOR AN EXPLANATION.
UNNHH...
I HAVE BEEN TRACKING THE MUTANT KNOWN AS SABRETOOTH FOR SEVERAL WEEKS IN AN ATTEMPT TO STOP HIM.
STOP HIM FROM WHAT? WHAT'S HE WANT?
HE WANTS TO HUNT.

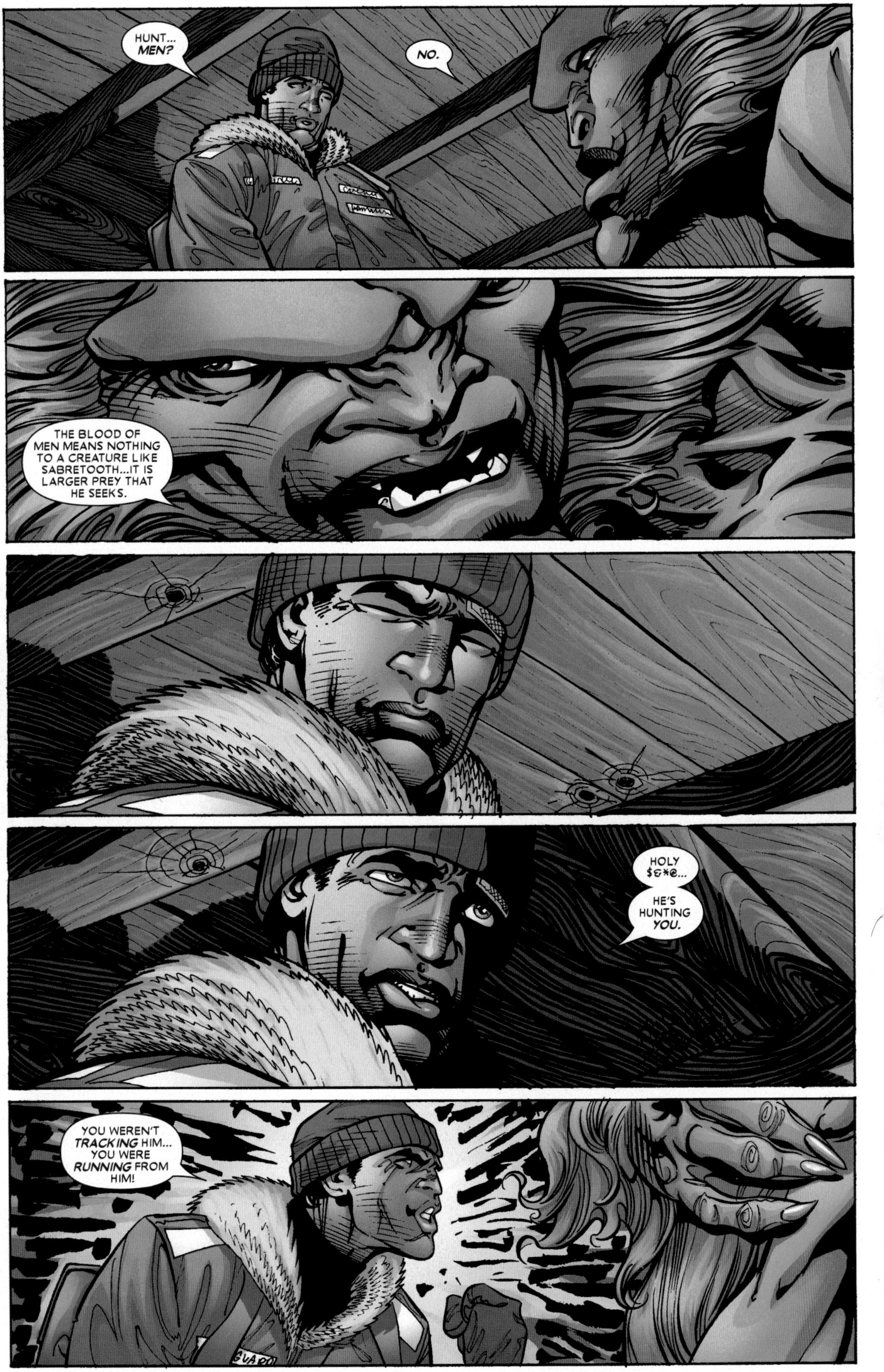
HUNT... *MEN?*
NO.
THE BLOOD OF MEN MEANS NOTHING TO A CREATURE LIKE SABRETOOTH...IT IS LARGER PREY THAT HE SEEKS.
HOLY $&*@... HE'S HUNTING *YOU.*
YOU WEREN'T *TRACKING* HIM... YOU WERE *RUNNING* FROM HIM!

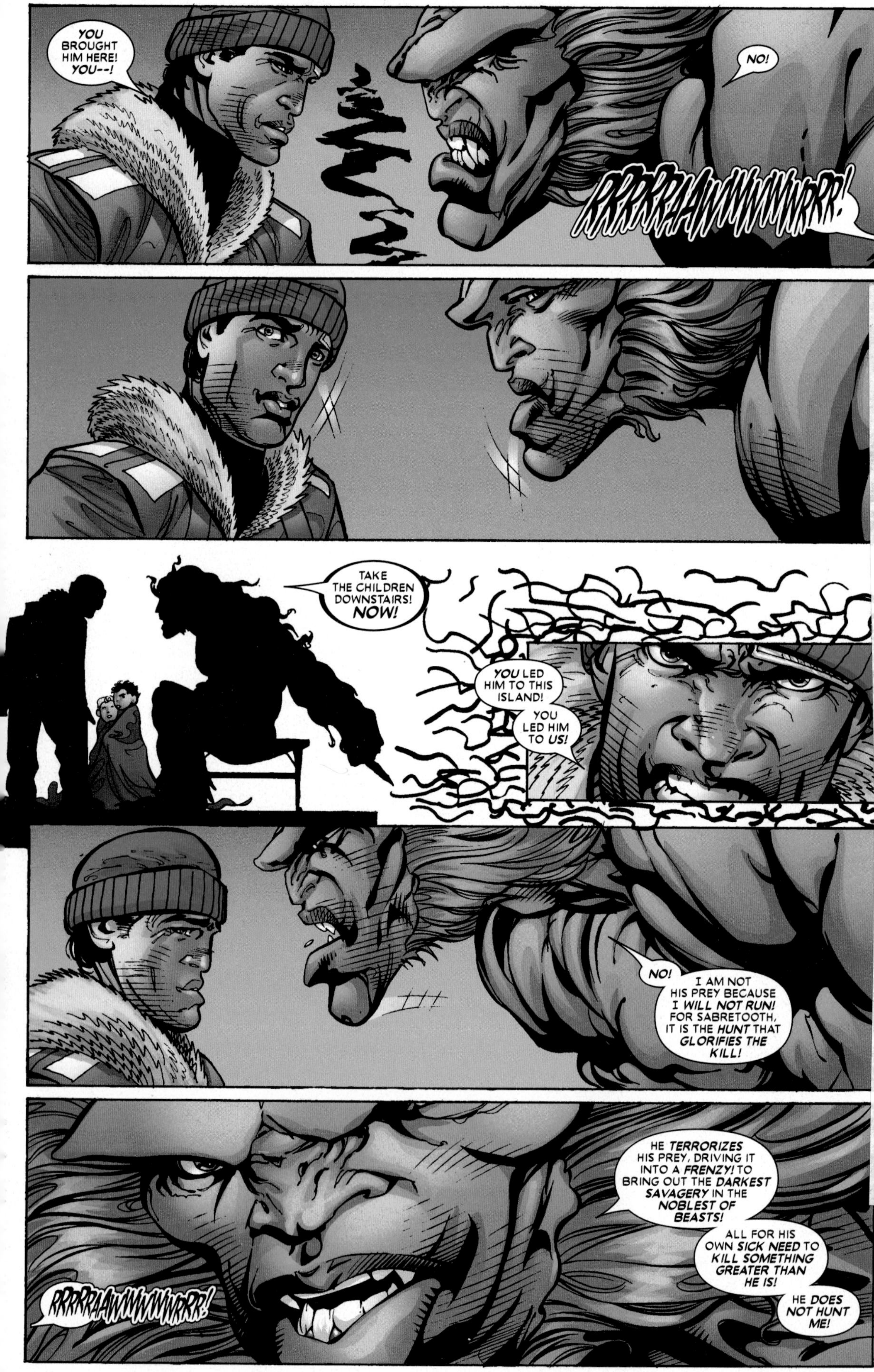
YOU BROUGHT HIM HERE! YOU--!
NO!
RRRRRRAAWWWWWRRR!
TAKE THE CHILDREN DOWNSTAIRS! NOW!
YOU LED HIM TO THIS ISLAND!
YOU LED HIM TO US!
NO!
I AM NOT HIS PREY BECAUSE I WILL NOT RUN! FOR SABRETOOTH, IT IS THE HUNT THAT GLORIFIES THE KILL!
HE TERRORIZES HIS PREY, DRIVING IT INTO A FRENZY! TO BRING OUT THE DARKEST SAVAGERY IN THE NOBLEST OF BEASTS!
ALL FOR HIS OWN SICK NEED TO KILL SOMETHING GREATER THAN HE IS!
HE DOES NOT HUNT ME!
RRRRRAAWWWWWRRR!

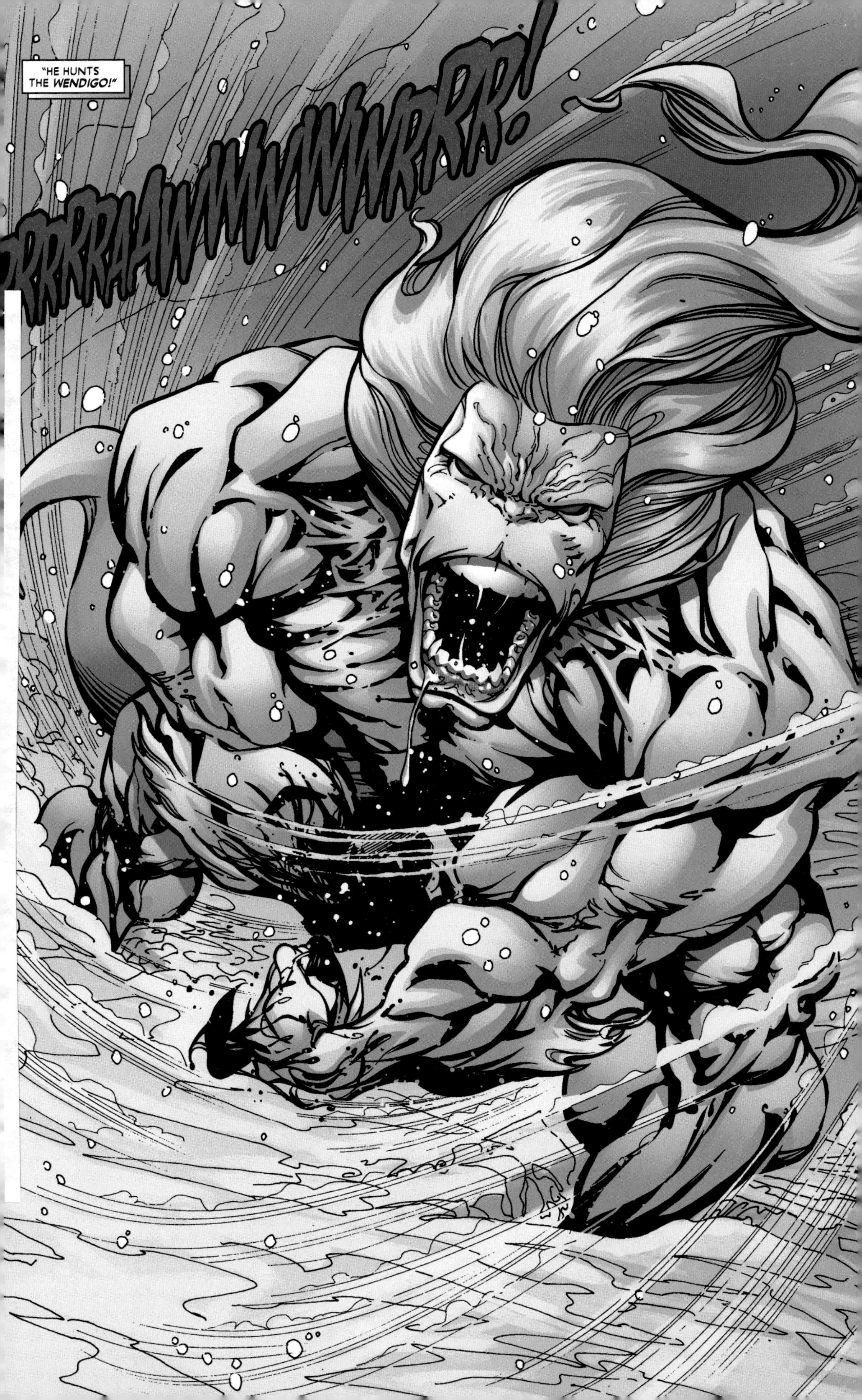
"HE HUNTS THE WENDIGO!"
RRRRAAWWWWWRRR!

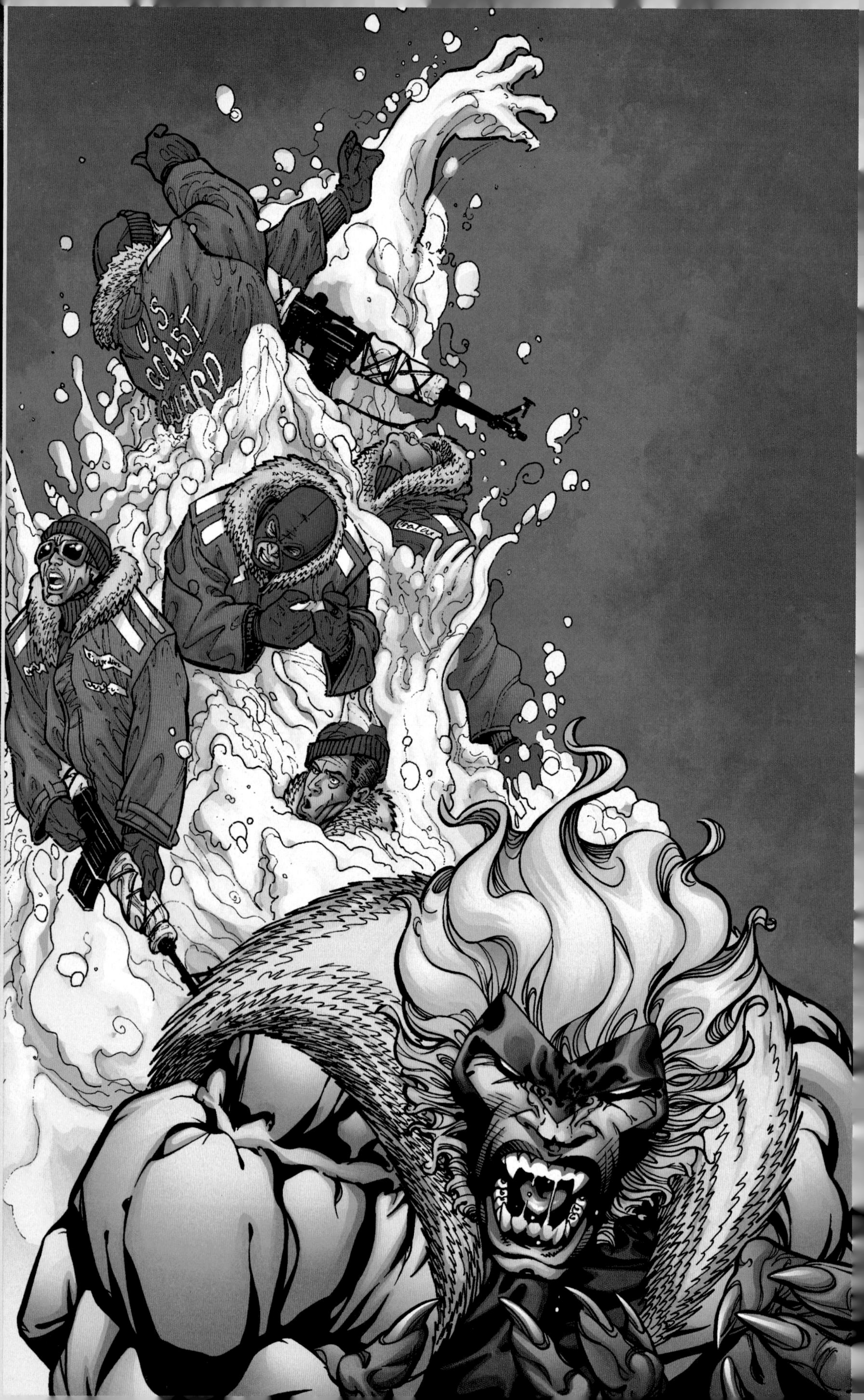
U.S. COAST GUARD

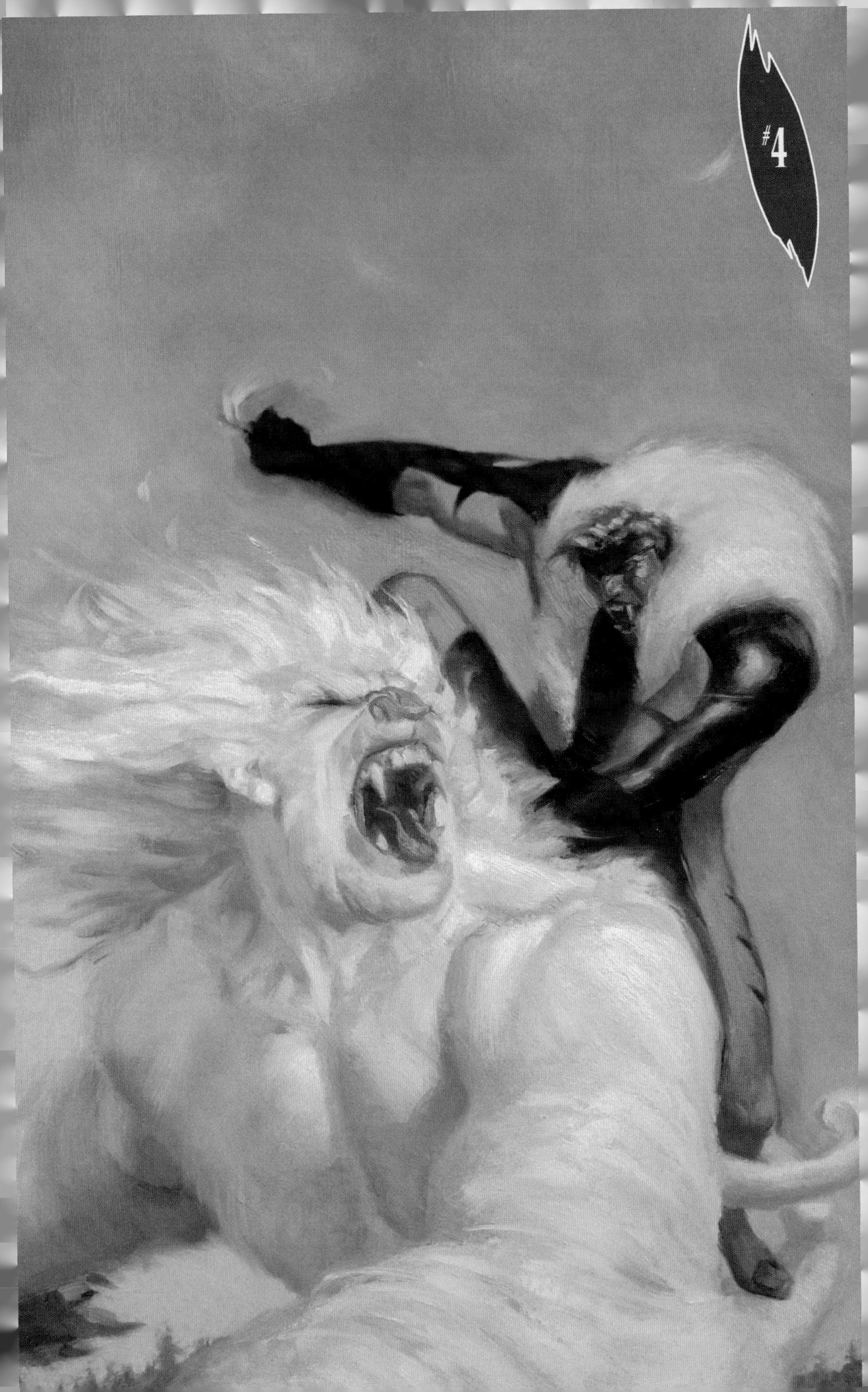
#4

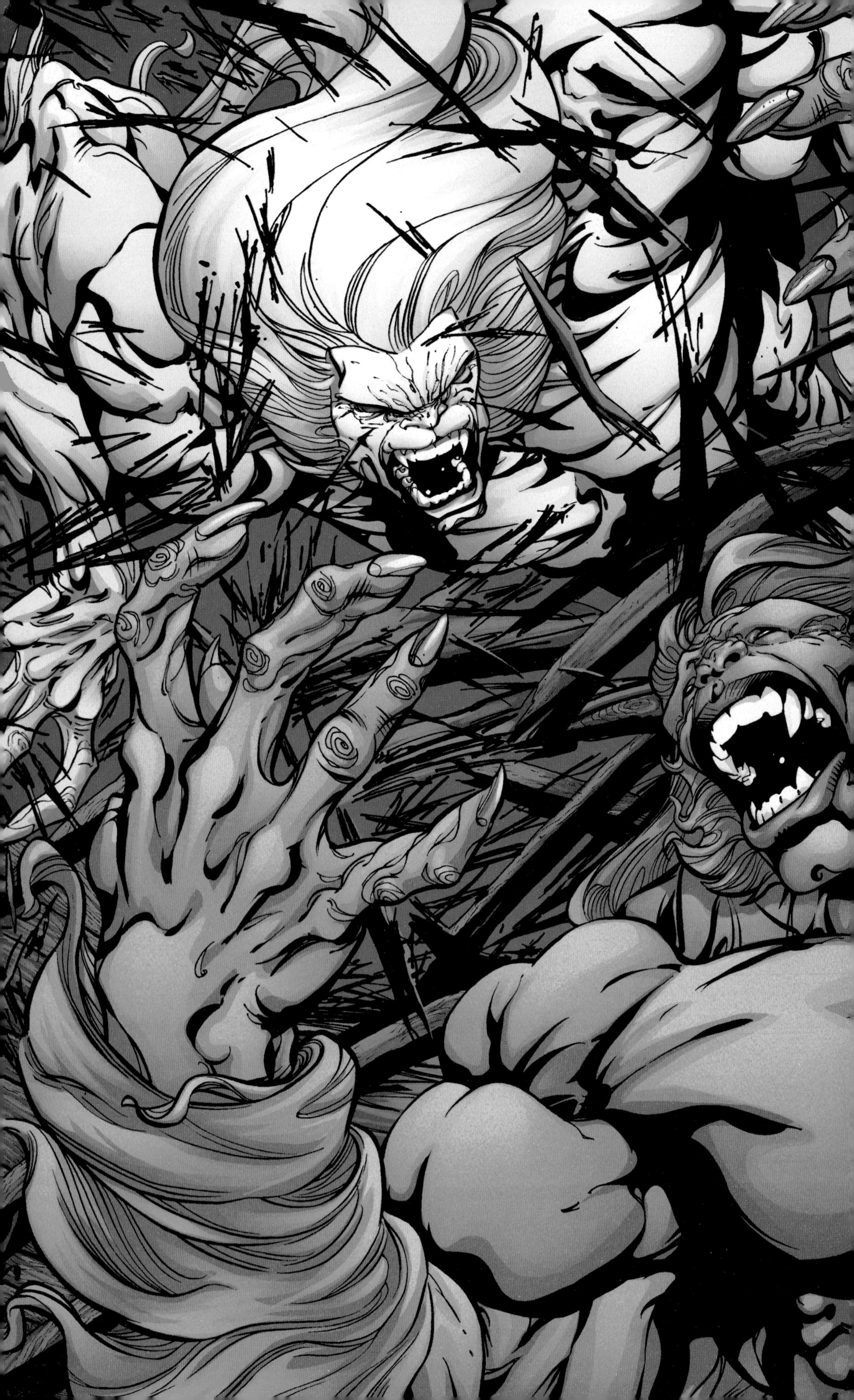

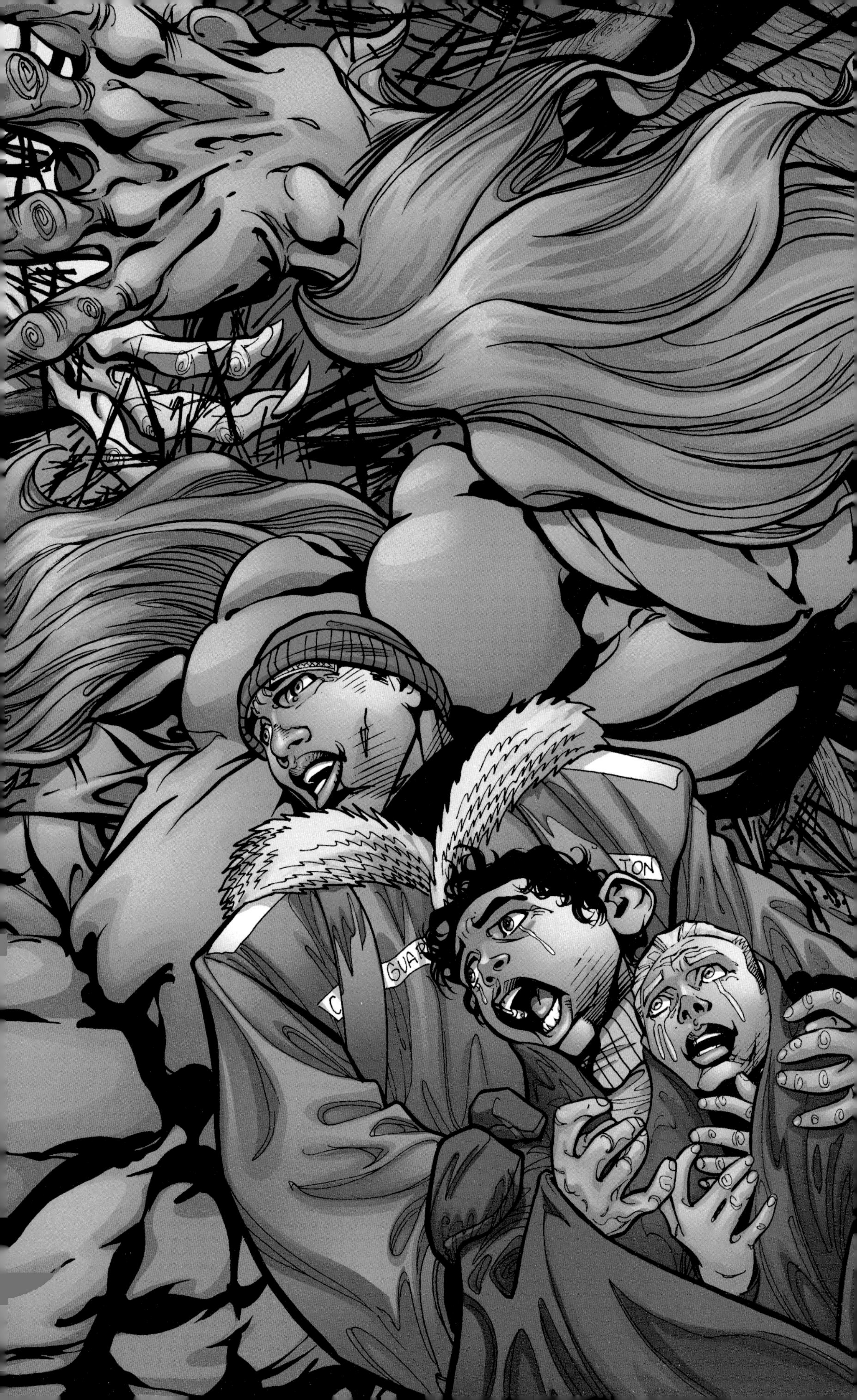

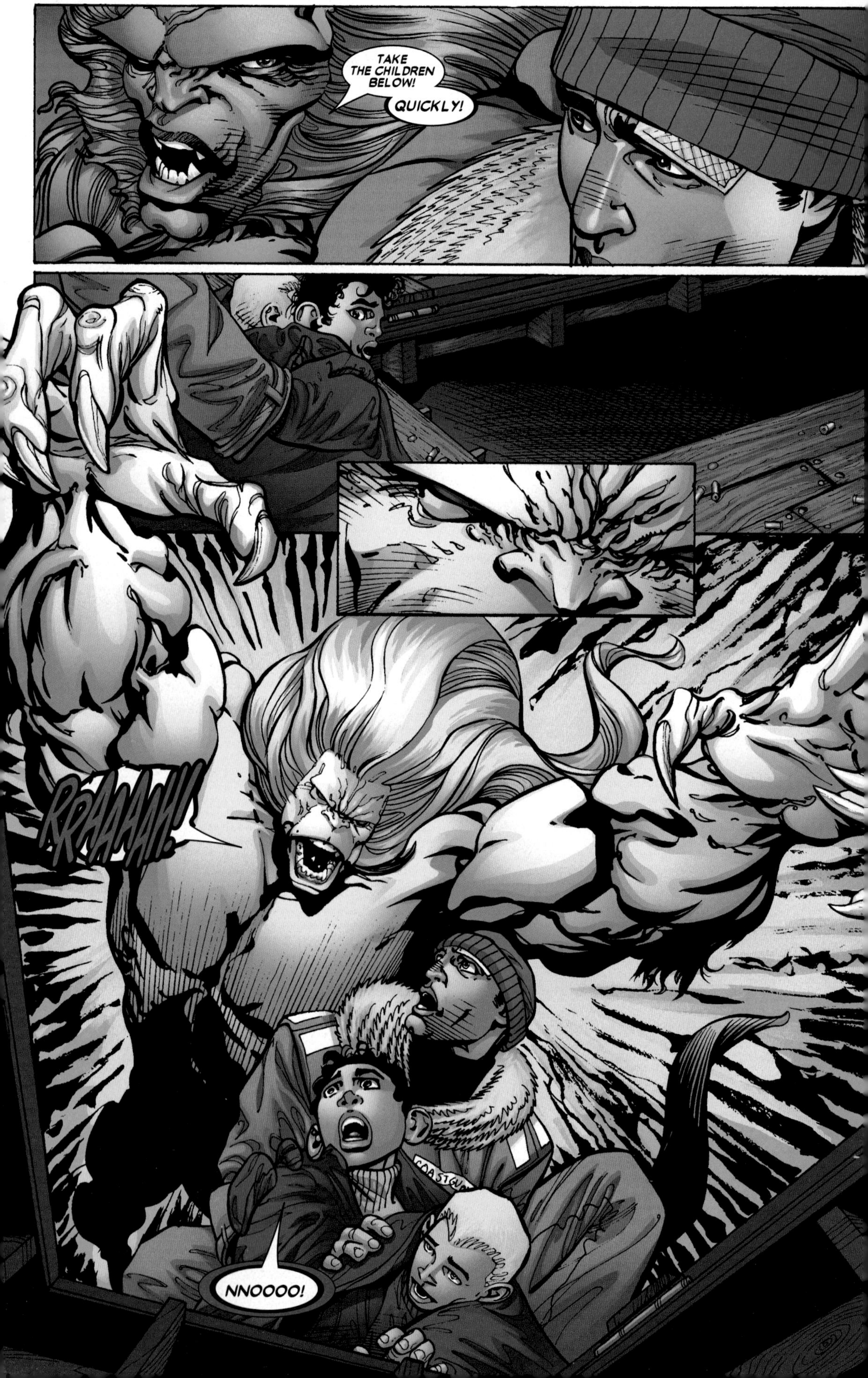
TAKE THE CHILDREN BELOW!
QUICKLY!
RRAAAAH!
NNOOOO!

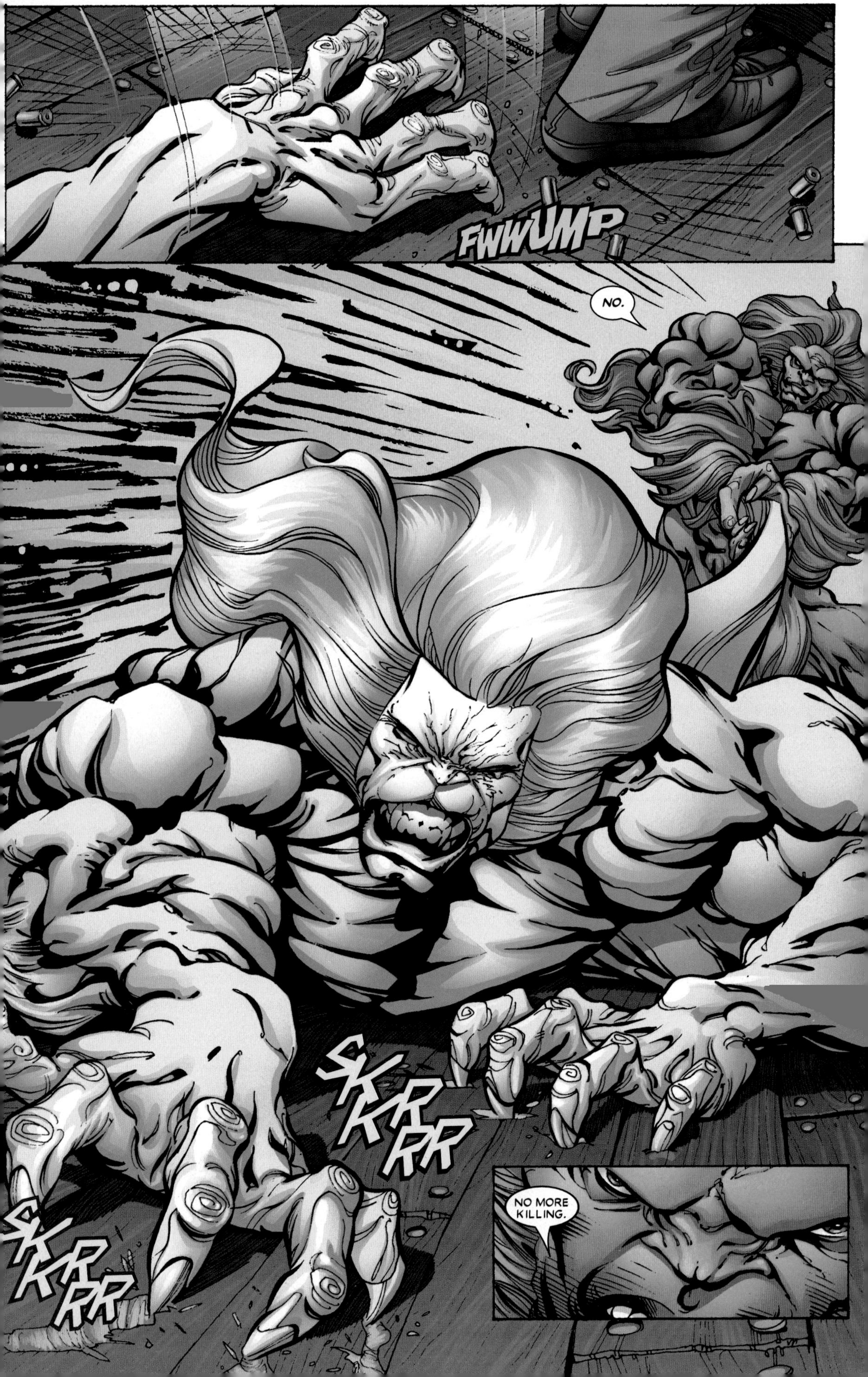
FWWUMP
NO.
SKRRR
SKRRR
NO MORE KILLING.

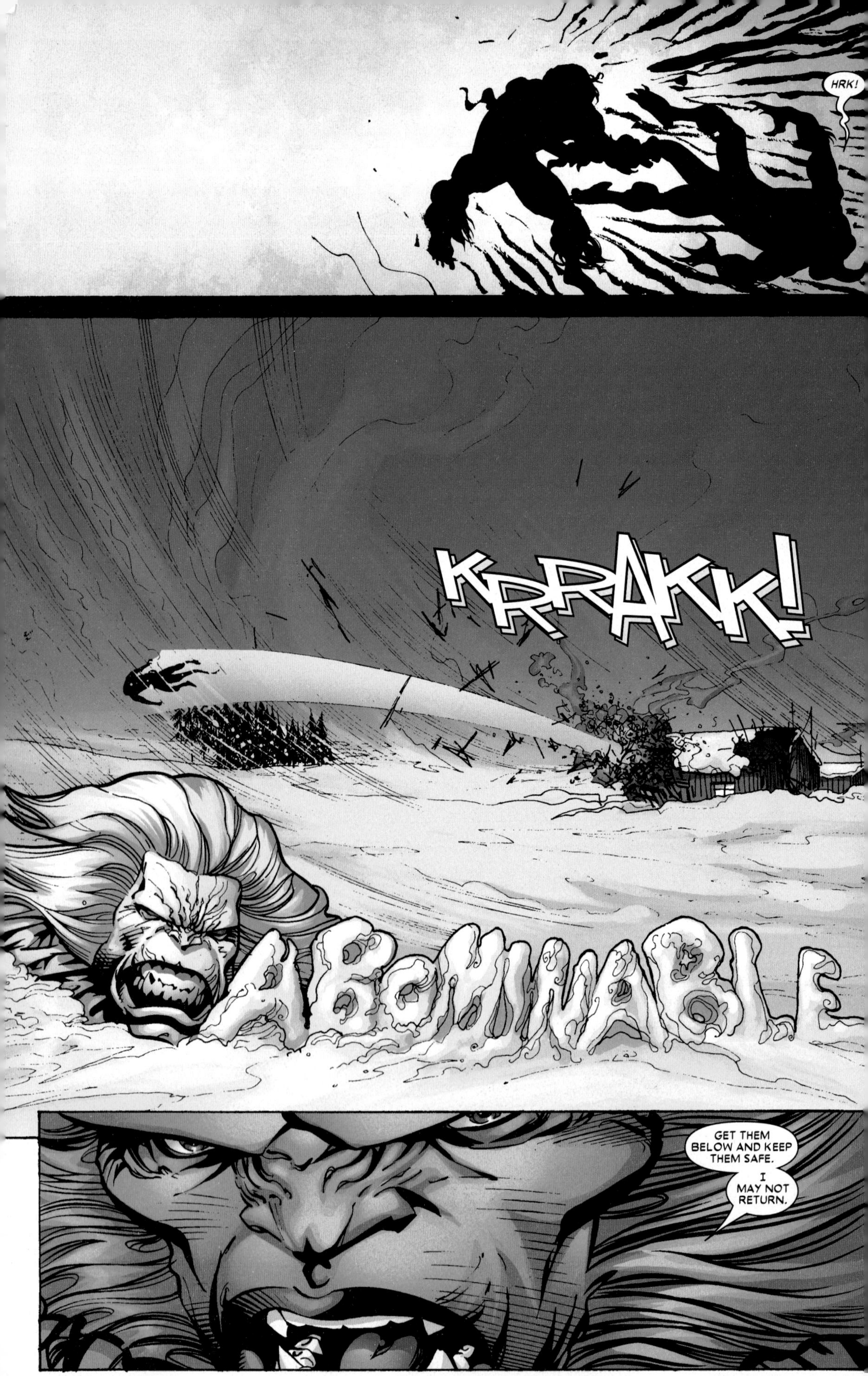
HRK!
KRRAKK!
ABOMINABLE
GET THEM BELOW AND KEEP THEM SAFE.
I MAY NOT RETURN.

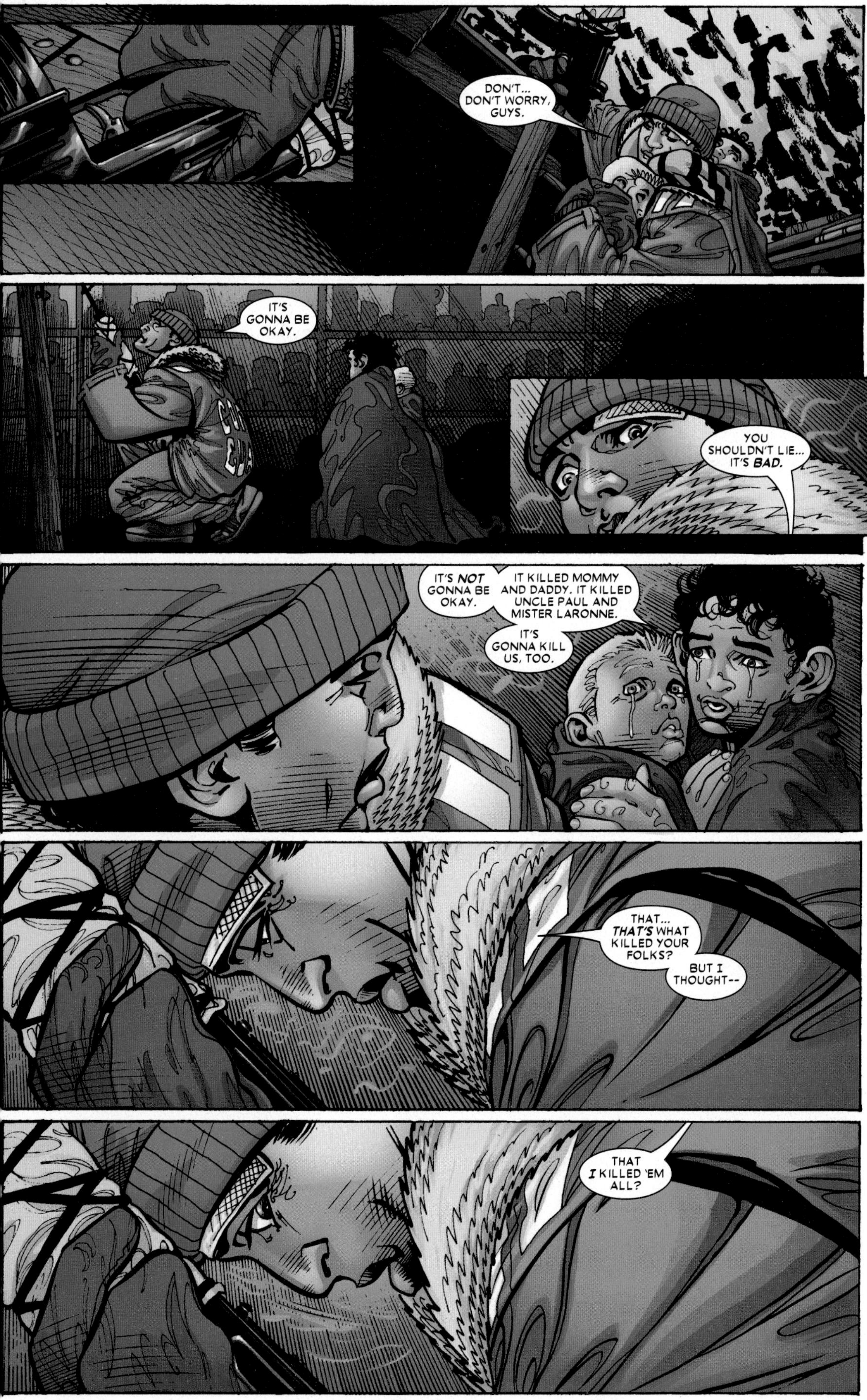
DON'T... DON'T WORRY, GUYS.
IT'S GONNA BE OKAY.
YOU SHOULDN'T LIE... IT'S *BAD.*
IT'S *NOT* GONNA BE OKAY.
IT KILLED MOMMY AND DADDY. IT KILLED UNCLE PAUL AND MISTER LARONNE.
IT'S GONNA KILL US, TOO.
THAT... *THAT'S* WHAT KILLED YOUR FOLKS?
BUT I THOUGHT--
THAT *I* KILLED 'EM ALL?

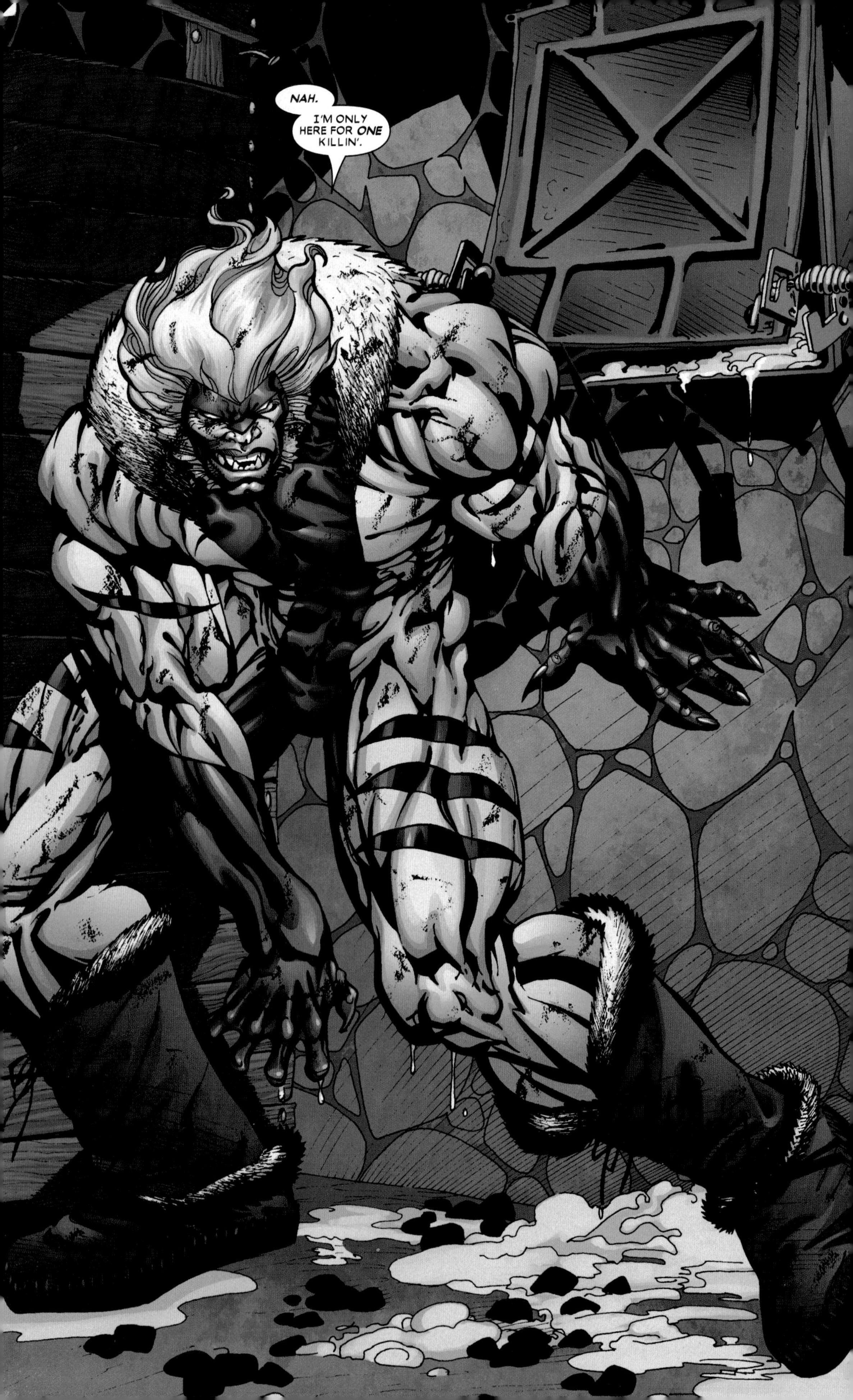
NAH.
I'M ONLY HERE FOR ONE KILLIN'.

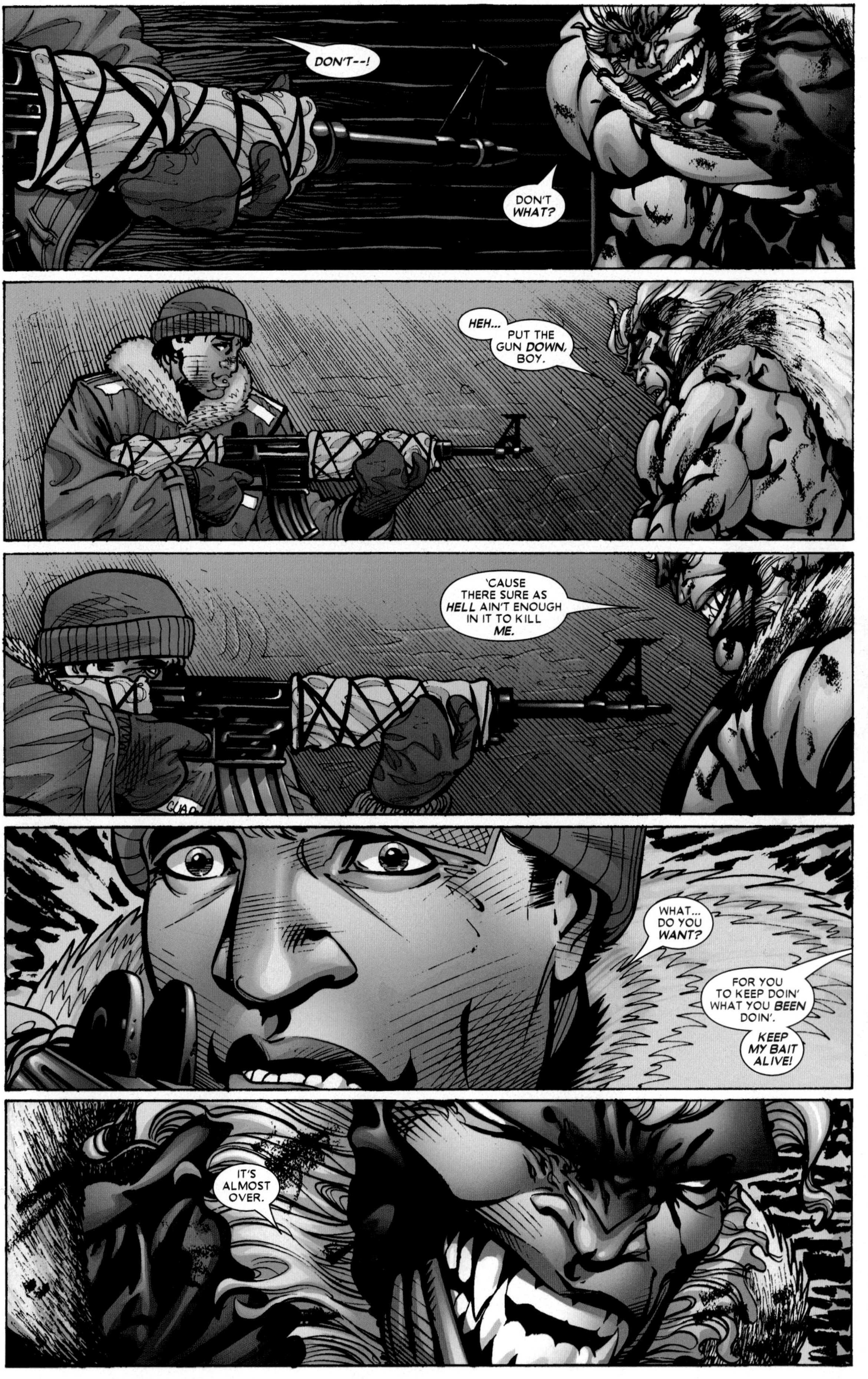
DON'T--!
DON'T WHAT?
HEH... PUT THE GUN DOWN, BOY.
'CAUSE THERE SURE AS HELL AIN'T ENOUGH IN IT TO KILL ME.
WHAT... DO YOU WANT?
FOR YOU TO KEEP DOIN' WHAT YOU BEEN DOIN'.
KEEP MY BAIT ALIVE!
IT'S ALMOST OVER.

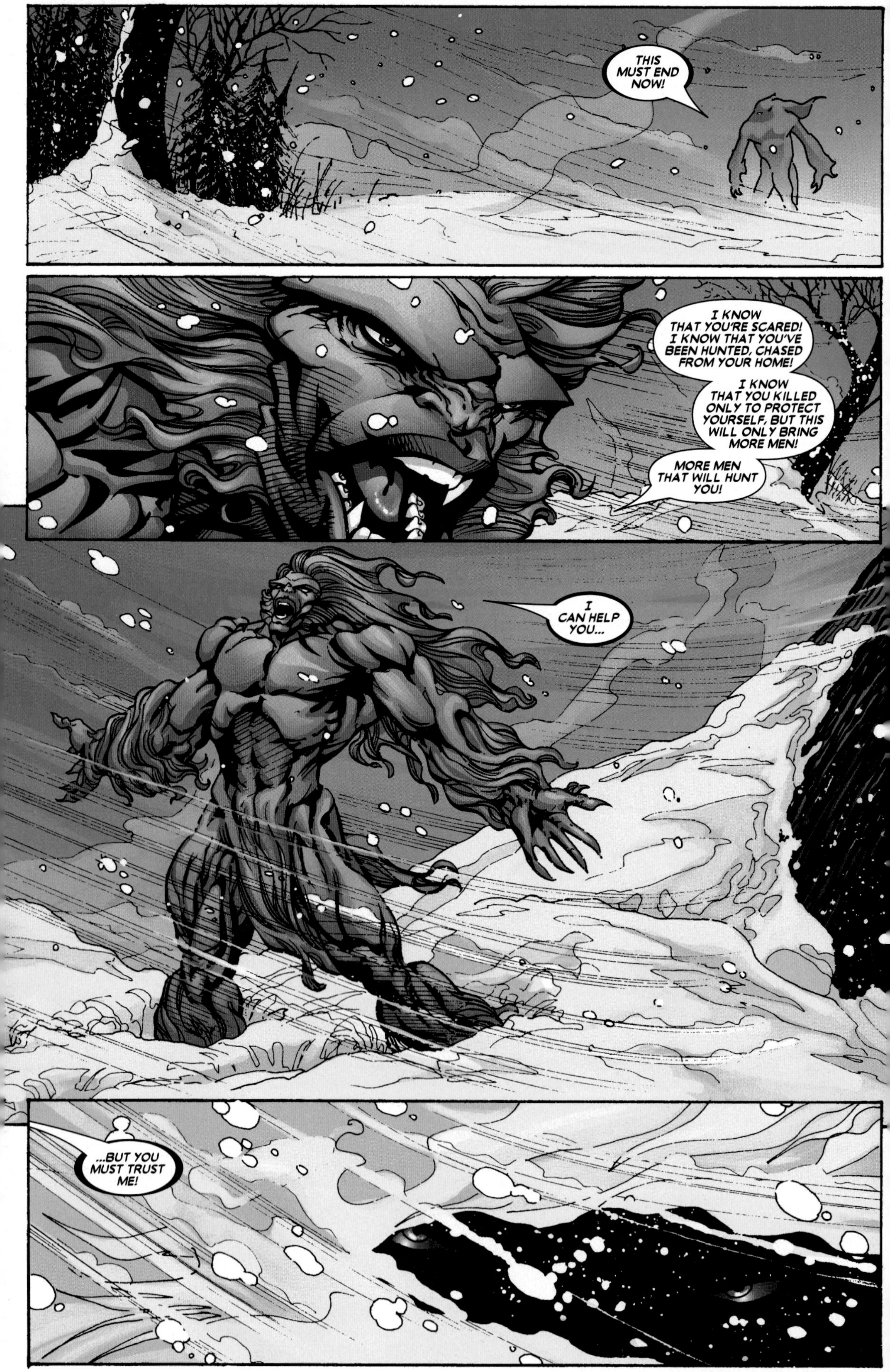
THIS MUST END NOW!
I KNOW THAT YOU'RE SCARED! I KNOW THAT YOU'VE BEEN HUNTED, CHASED FROM YOUR HOME!
I KNOW THAT YOU KILLED ONLY TO PROTECT YOURSELF, BUT THIS WILL ONLY BRING MORE MEN!
MORE MEN THAT WILL HUNT YOU!
I CAN HELP YOU...
...BUT YOU MUST TRUST ME!

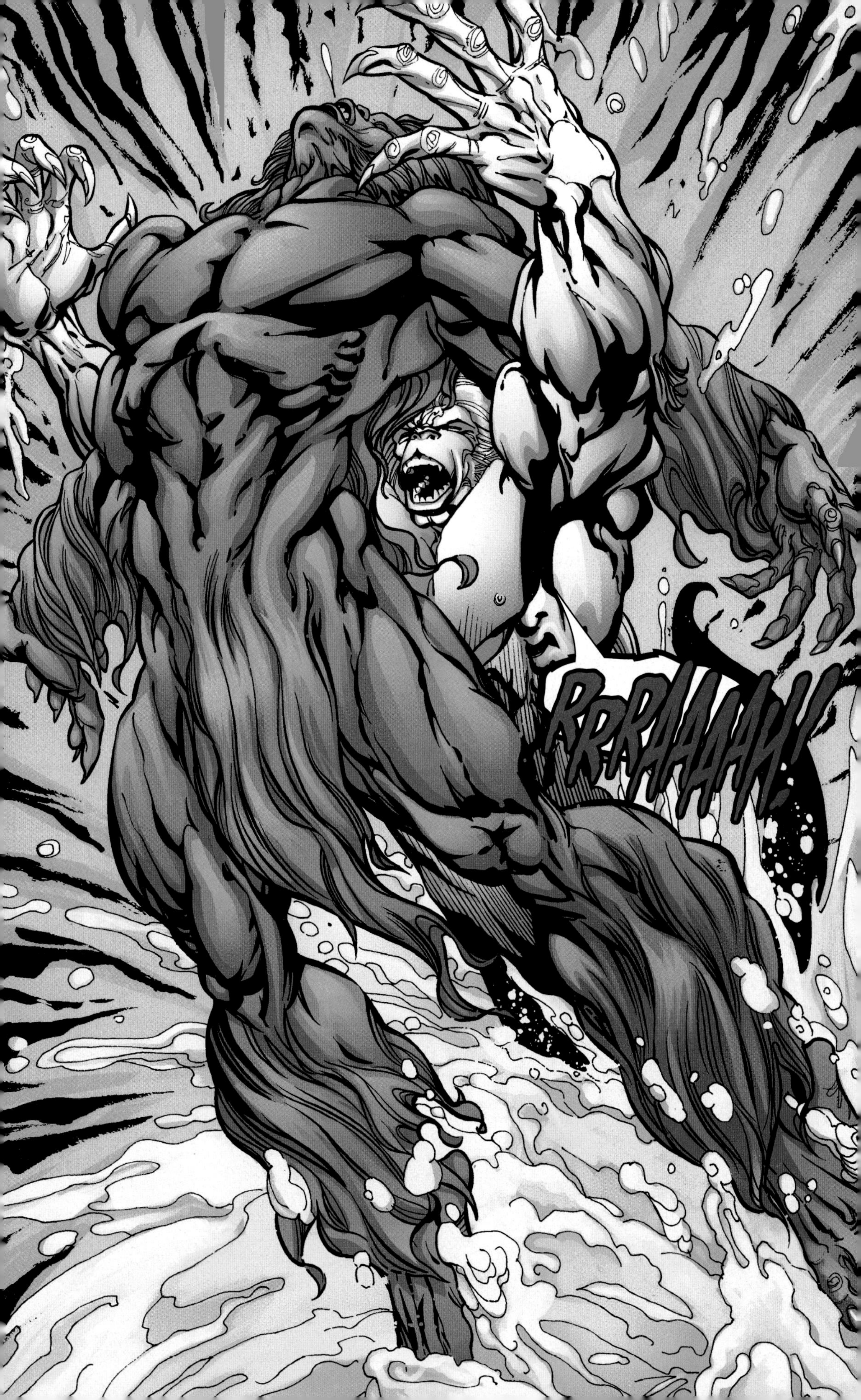
RRRAAAAH!

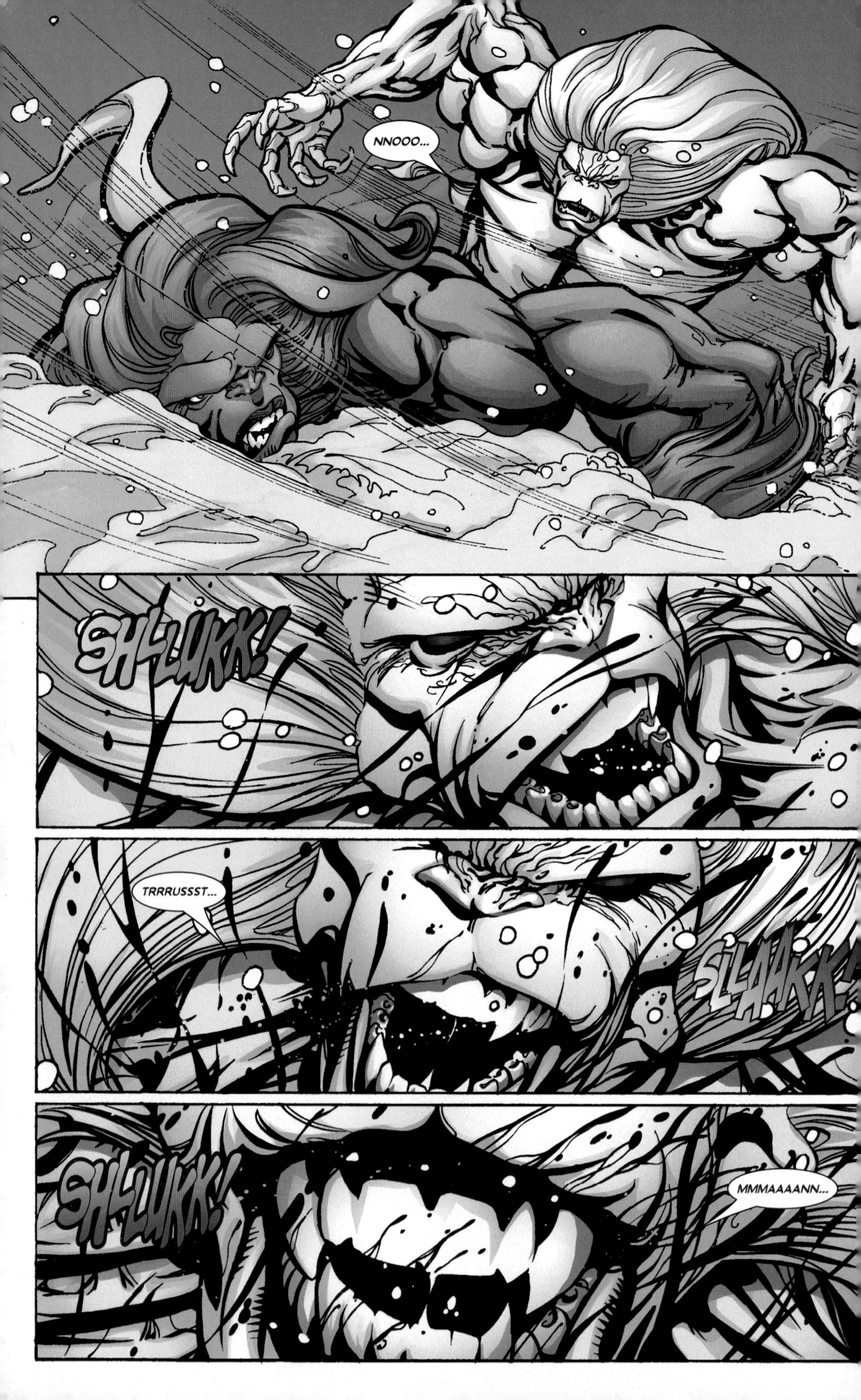
NNOOO...
SHLUKK!
TRRRUSSST...
SLAAKK
SHLUKK!
MMMAAAANN...

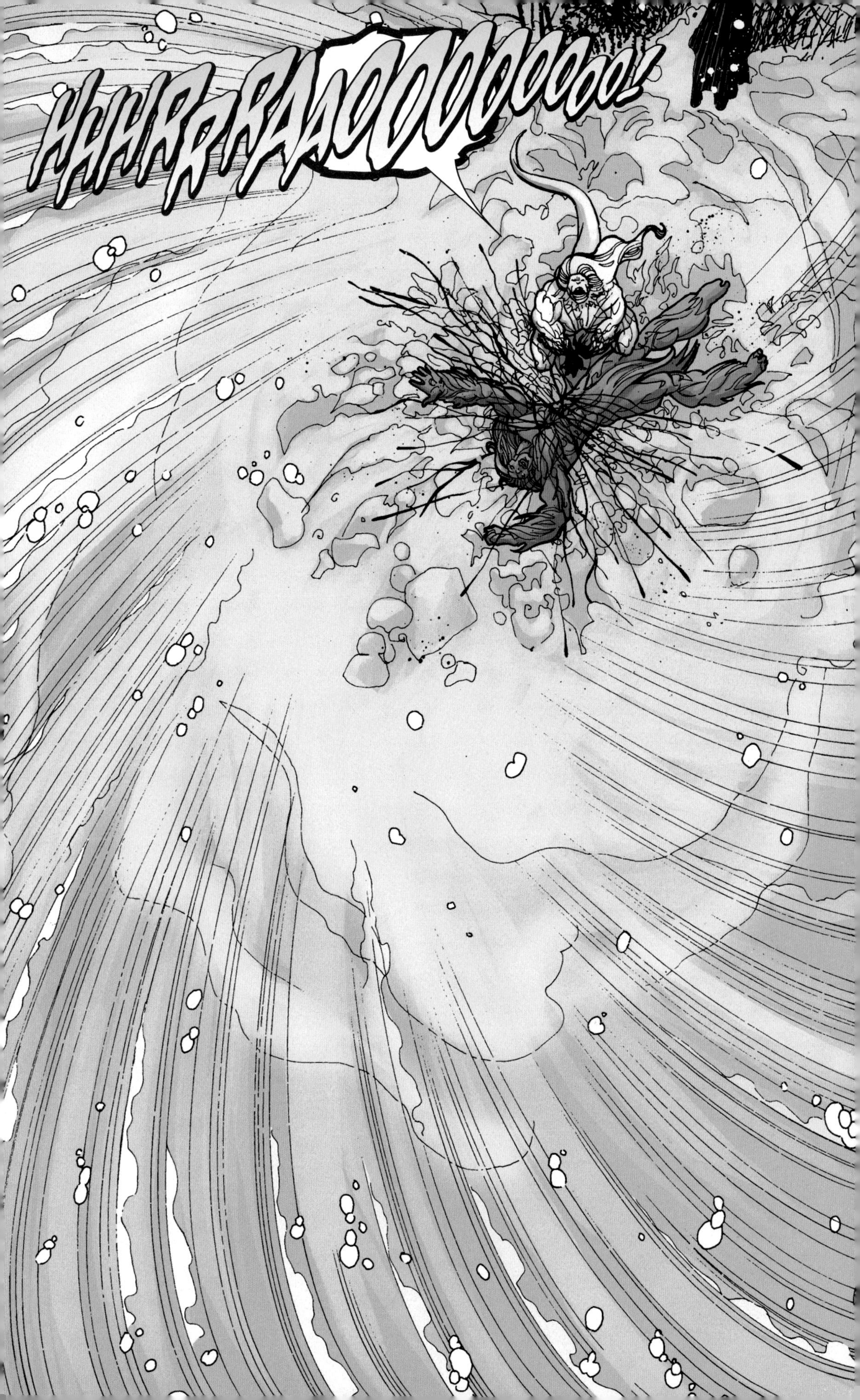
HUHRRAAOOOOOOOOO!

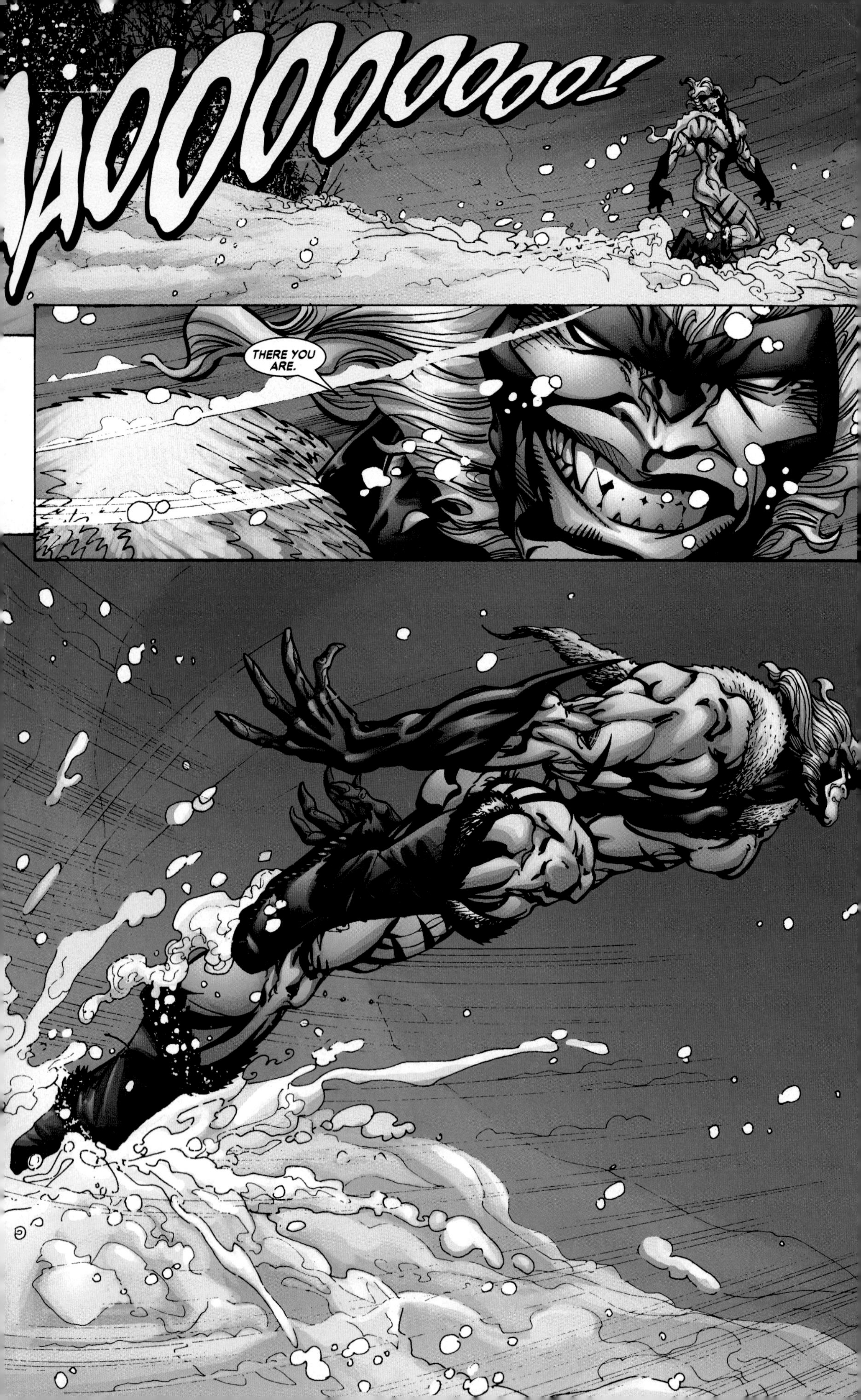
AOOOOOOO!
THERE YOU ARE.

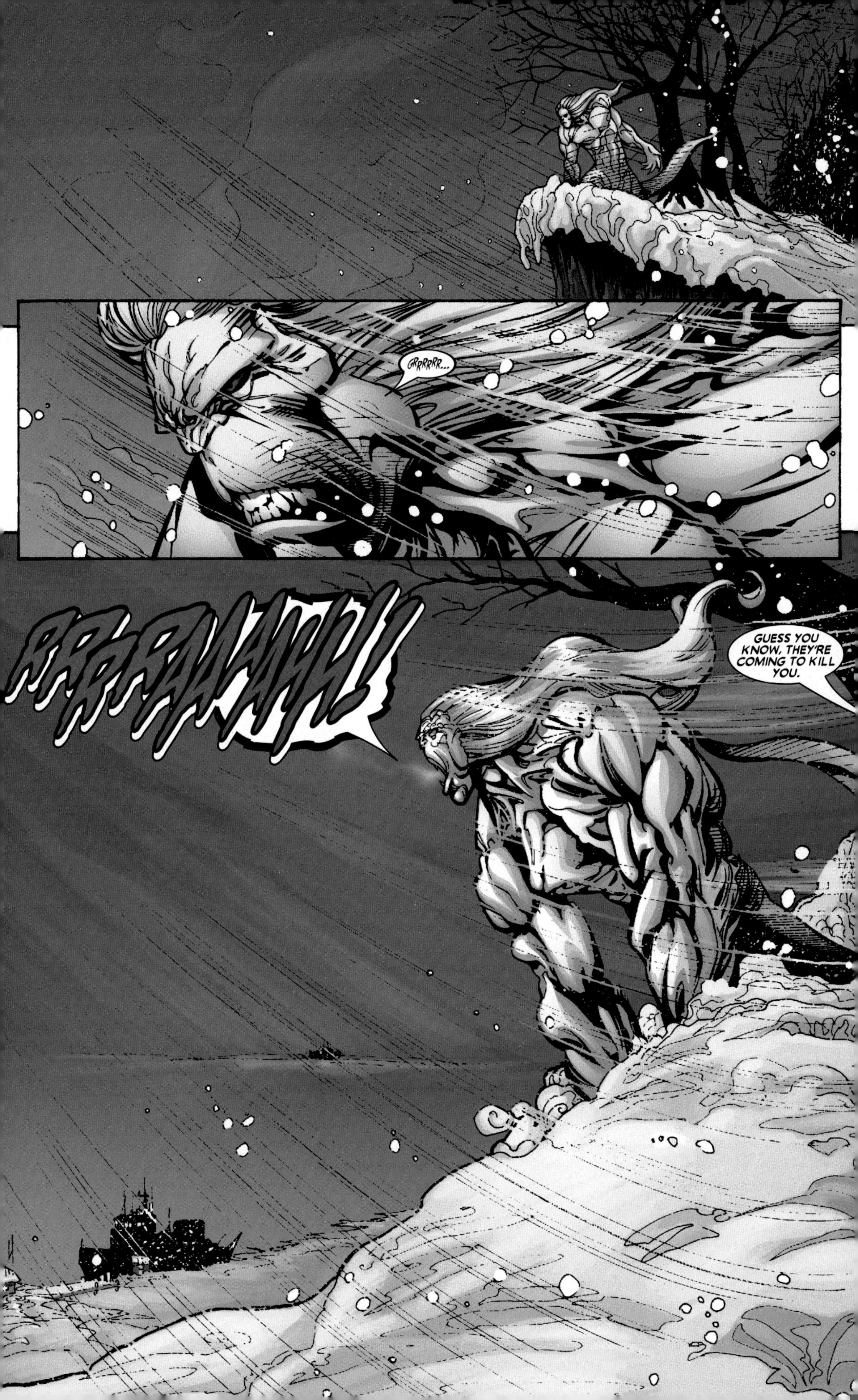
GRRRRRR...
RRRRAAAAAHH!
GUESS YOU KNOW, THEY'RE COMING TO KILL YOU.

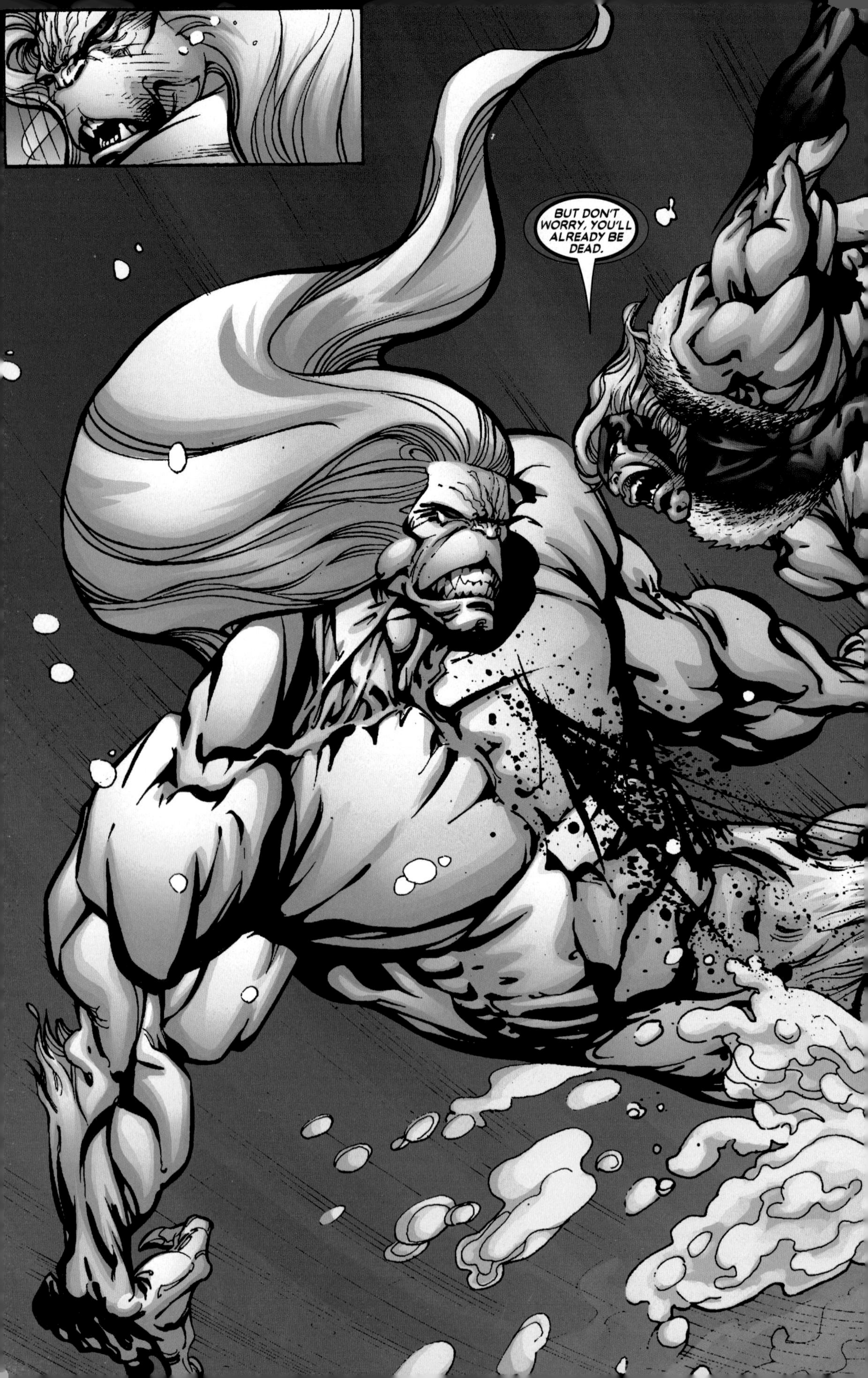
BUT DON'T WORRY, YOU'LL ALREADY BE DEAD.

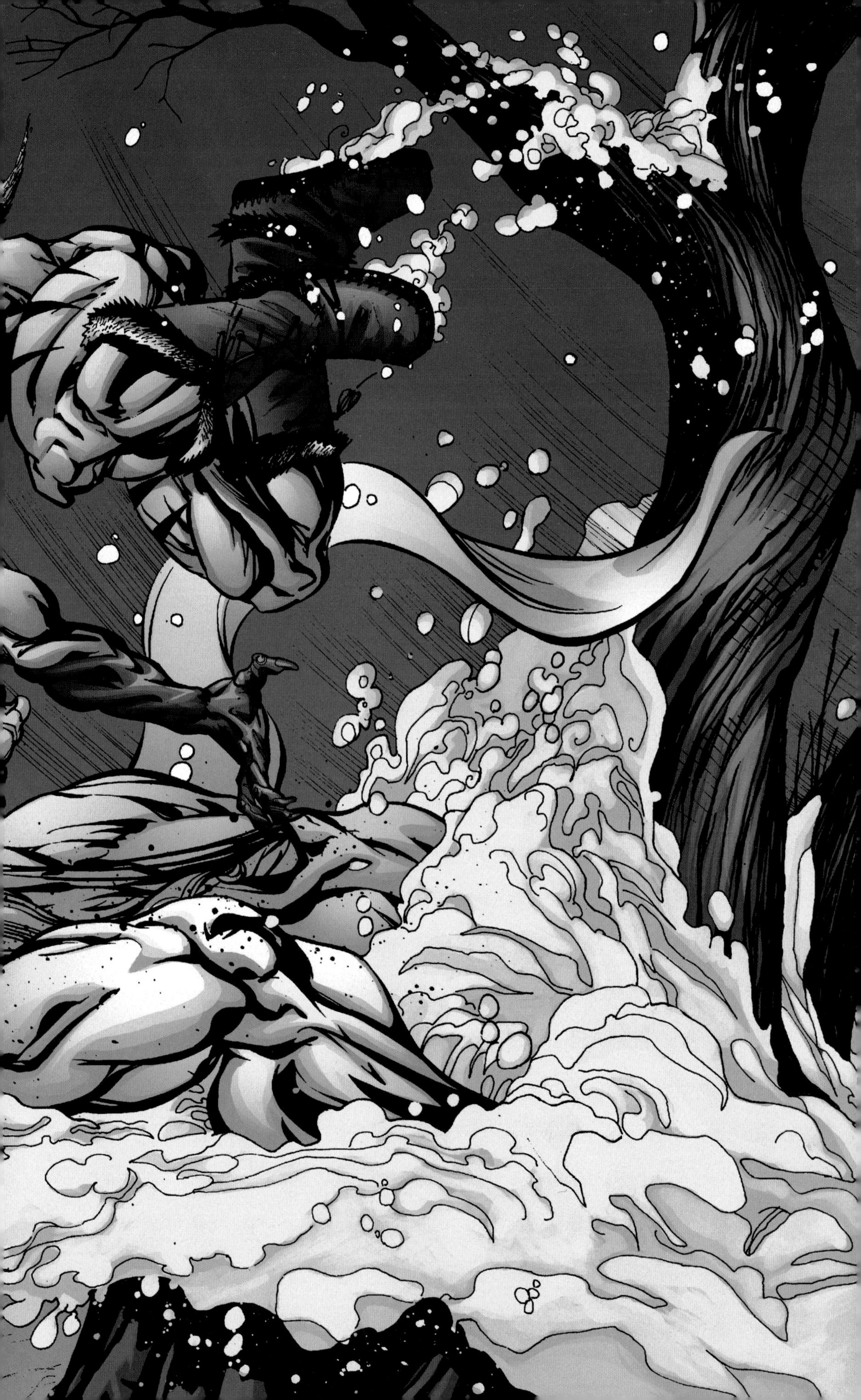

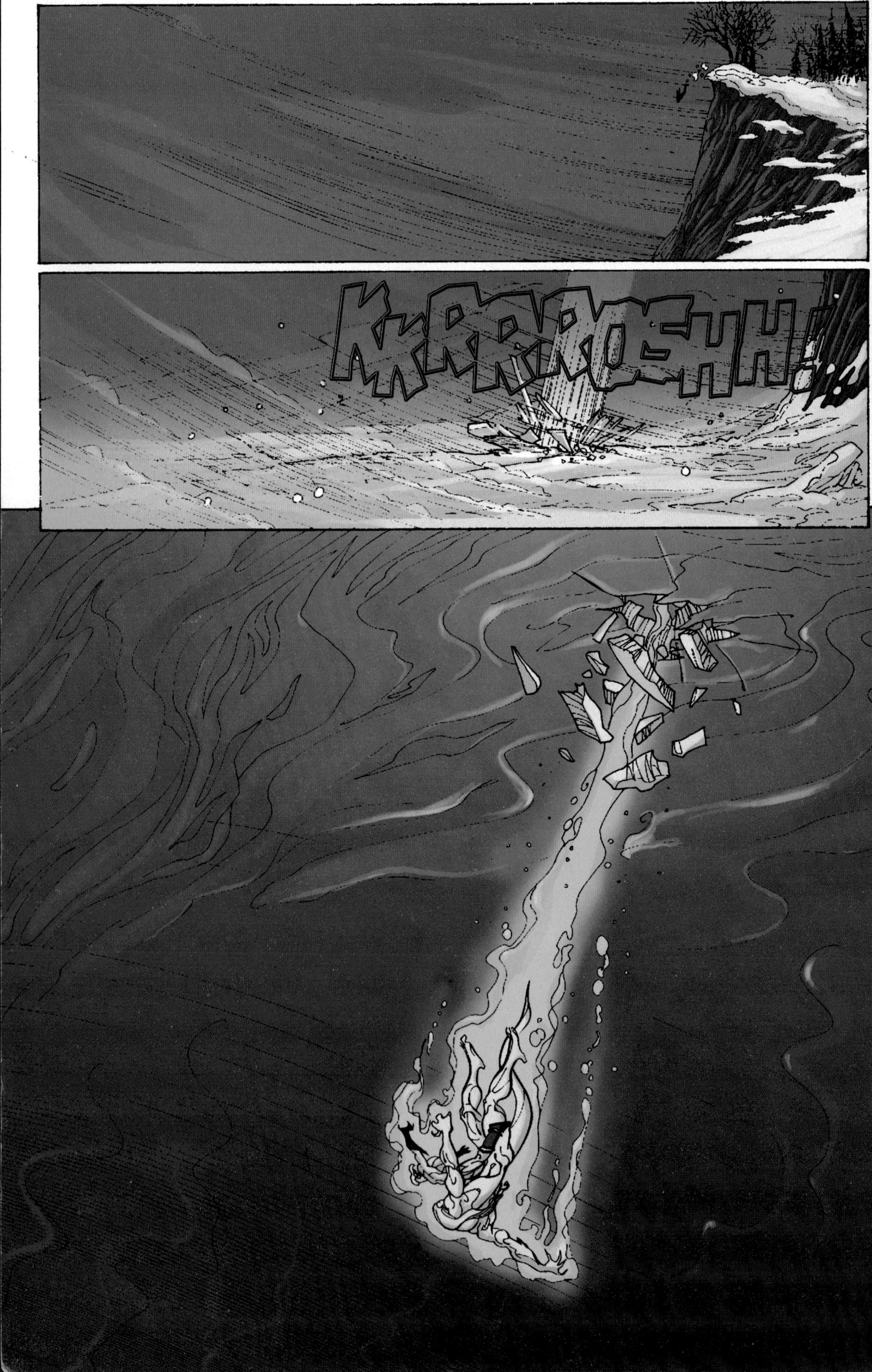
KKRRRROSHH!!

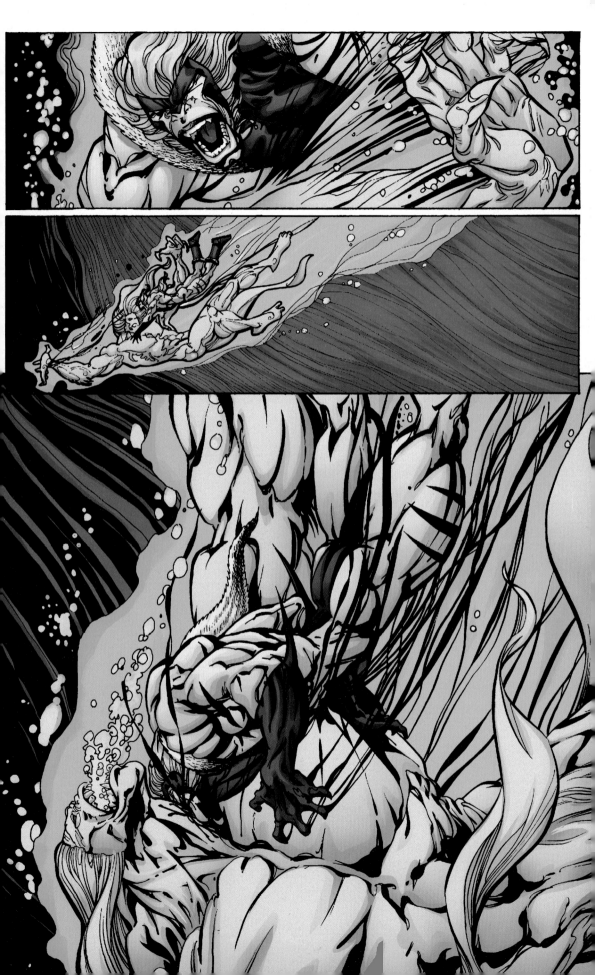

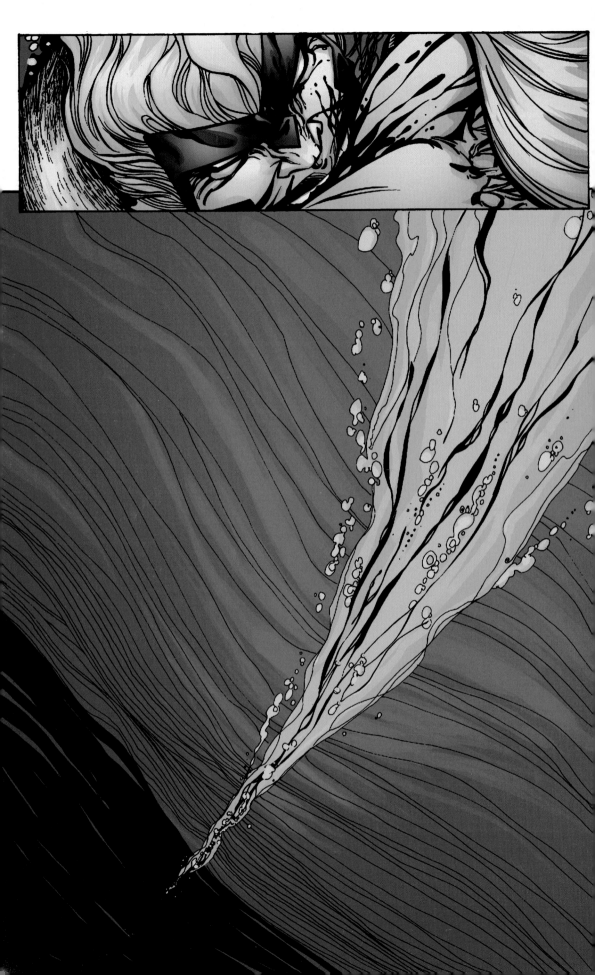

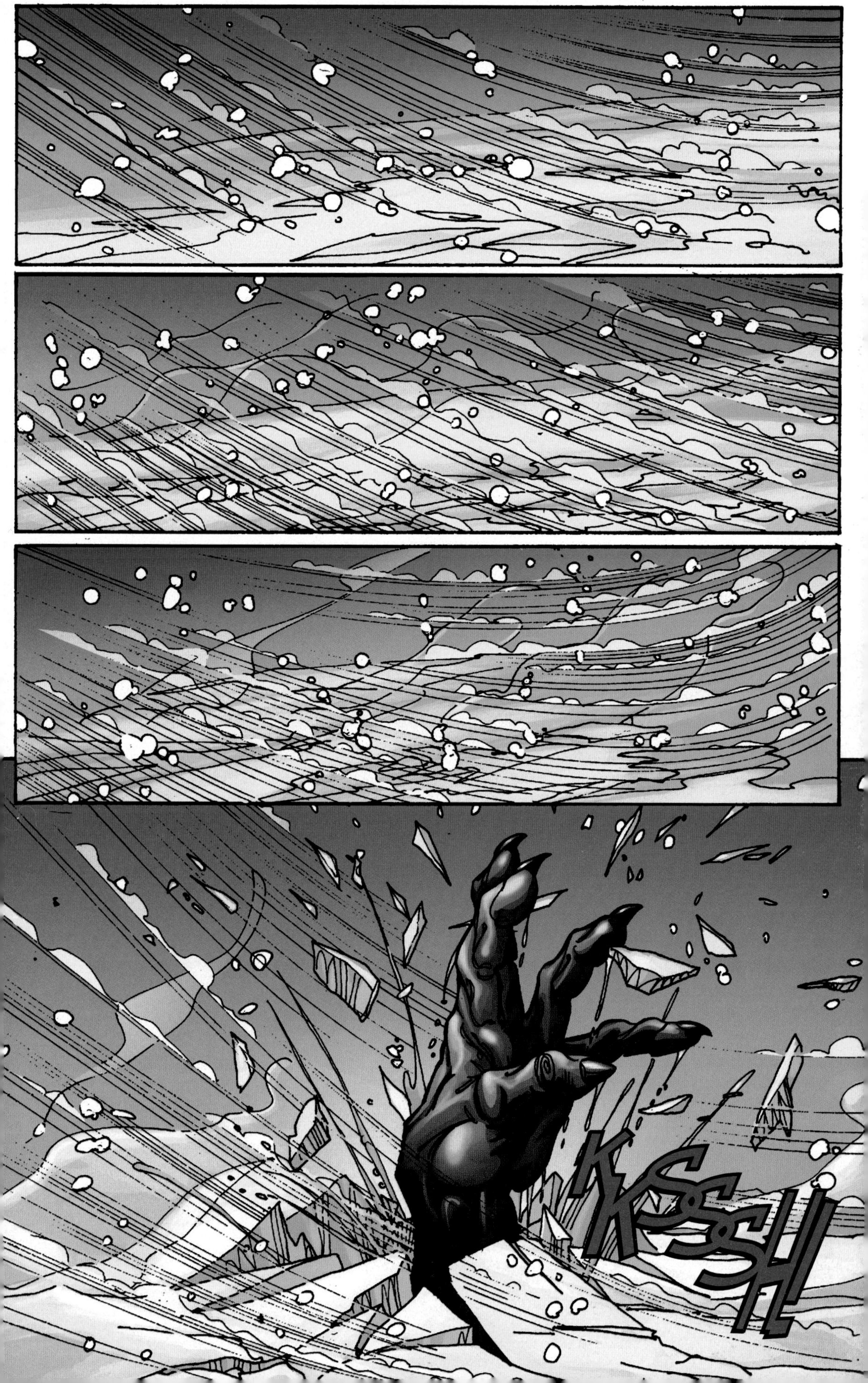
KKSSH!

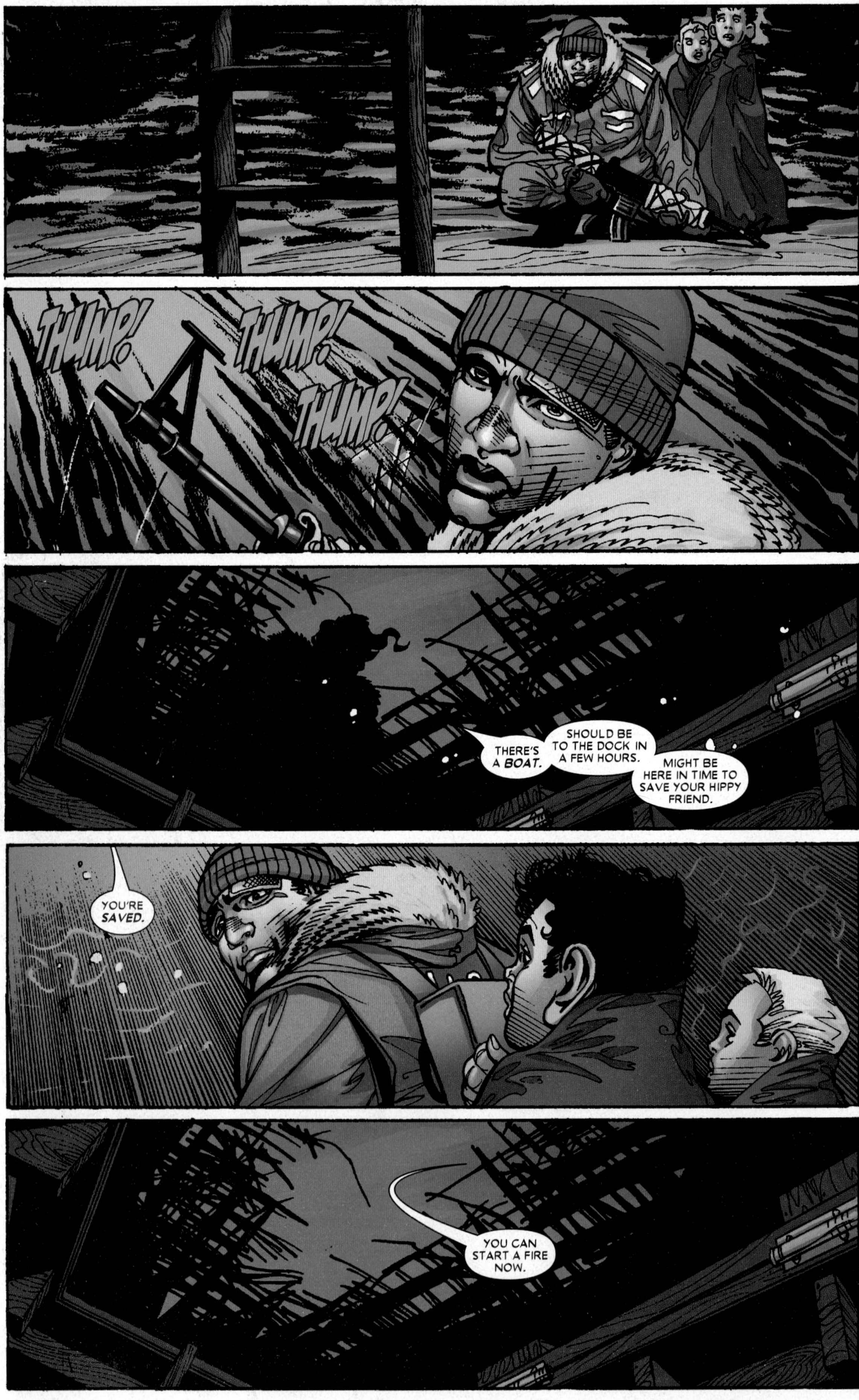
THUMP! THUMP! THUMP!
THERE'S A BOAT.
SHOULD BE TO THE DOCK IN A FEW HOURS.
MIGHT BE HERE IN TIME TO SAVE YOUR HIPPY FRIEND.
YOU'RE SAVED.
YOU CAN START A FIRE NOW.

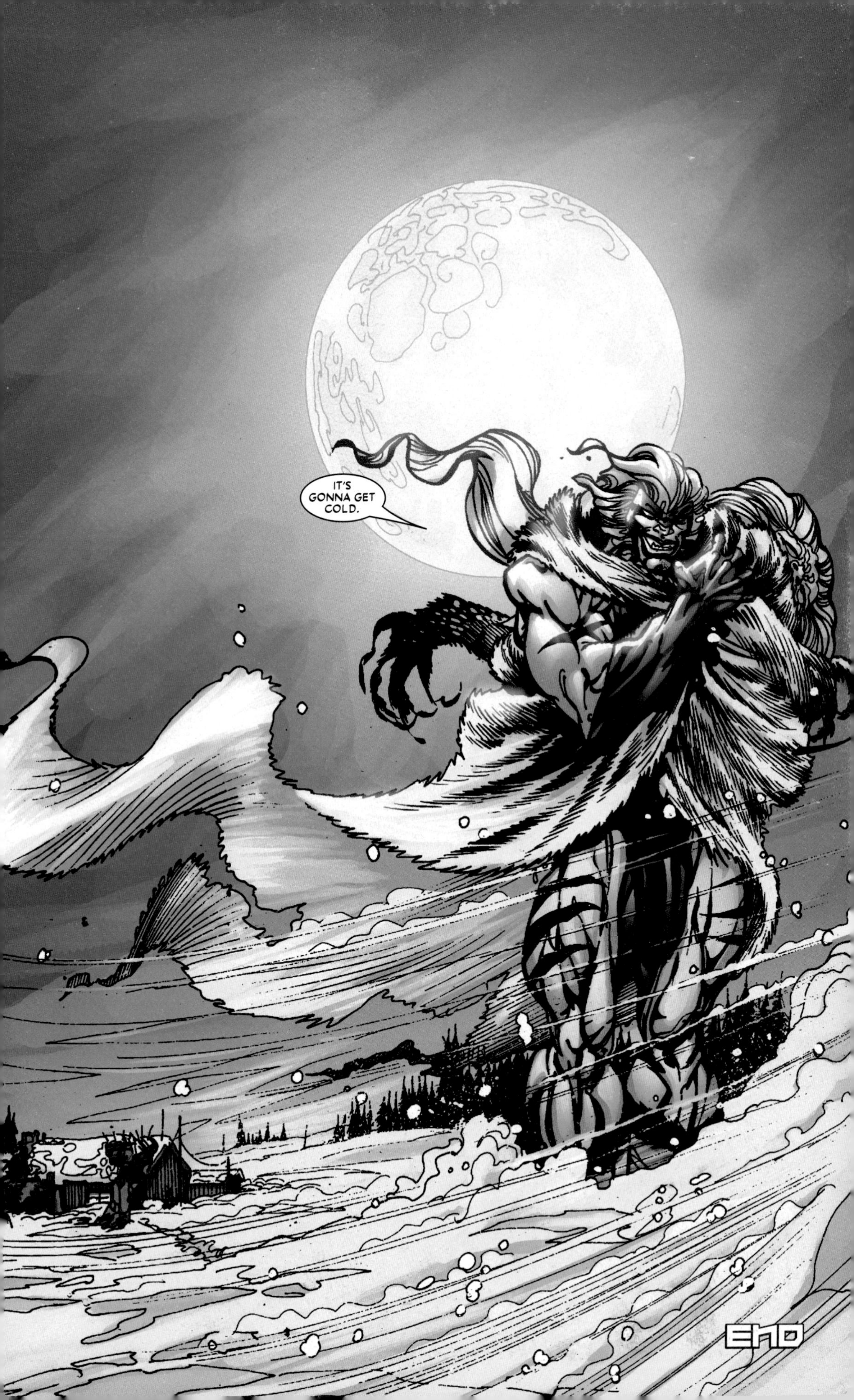
IT'S GONNA GET COLD.
END

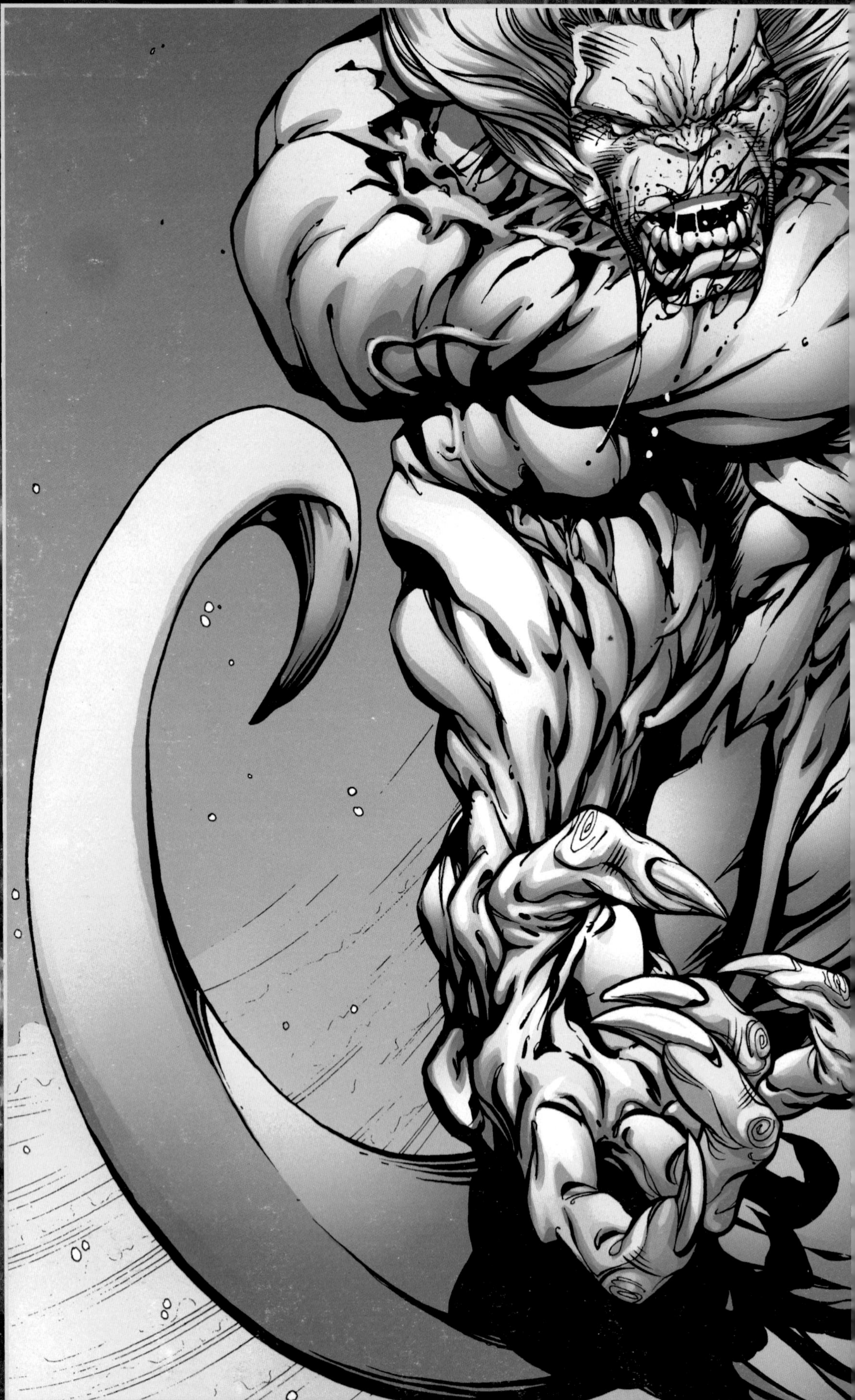